the CRESCENT and the CROSS

the CRESCENT and the CROSS

DAN THEIS

Publishers since 1798

THOMAS NELSON INC., PUBLISHERS

Nashville   New York

First edition

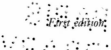

Library of Congress Cataloging in Publication Data

Theis, Dan.
  The crescent and the cross.

  Bibliography: p. 169
  Includes index.
  1. Crusades—First, 1096–1099. 2. Crusades—
Second, 1147–1149. 3. Crusades—Third, 1189–1192.
I. Title.
D161.2.T48   940.1′8   78–2385
ISBN 0–8407–6596–7

contents

The Rulers of Jerusalem

Ruler	Right of succession	Reign
Godfrey (of Bouillon)		*1099–1100*
Baldwin I (of Boulogne)	Brother of Godfrey	*1100–1118*
Baldwin II (of Le Bourg)	Cousin of Godfrey and Baldwin I	*1118–31*
Melisinde, heiress	Daughter of Baldwin II	*1131–52*
Fulk (of Anjou)	Married to Melisinde	*1131–43*
Baldwin III	Son of Melisinde and Fulk	*1143–63*
Amalric I	Brother of Baldwin III	*1163–74*
Baldwin IV	Son of Amalric I	*1174–85*
Baldwin V	Nephew of Baldwin IV	*1185–86*
Sibylla, heiress	Daughter of Amalric, mother of Baldwin V	*1186–90*
Guy (of Lusignan)	Married to Sibylla	*1186–92*
Isabella I, heiress	Sister of Sibylla	*1192–1205*
Conrad (of Montferrat)	Married to Isabella	*April 1192*

Through Isabella, the kings of Jerusalem continued to rule from Acre.

PART ONE

"GOD WILLS IT!"

1

the pope at clermont

It was cold that gray November day in the year of our Lord 1095. The sun had scattered the morning mist from the hills west of the town, but the light was pale and did not warm the hard ground. A smell of frost hung over the fields.

The crowd gathered near the raised platform outside the city gates milled and stamped like penned cattle before a storm. Some of them spoke in hushed whispers, because this was a solemn occasion. Others shouted happily because it was more like a holiday. No one seemed to notice the cold. They were burning with excitement.

The pope himself, Urban II, had come to Clermont (Clermont-Ferrand) in central France.

They were a mixed group who waited for Urban to come through the gates and take his place on the platform. There were cardinals and bishops, along with black-robed monks and a scattering of nobles. There were women, and children who clung to their mothers or chased each other through the crowd and added to the confusion. And there were the men—serfs from the surrounding countryside, dressed in shabby clothes that offset the bright finery of the churchmen.

9

They had come because the pope had called them—the bishops first to a great council, and the people to a public gathering. The council had ended after ten days, with only the solemn expressions of the priests and whispered rumors to warn the people that something momentous was stirring. Now a decision had been made. But a decision on what?

Certainly Urban had plenty on his mind. There was a false pope occupying the papal chair in Rome. The Church was split, fragmented, and in some places utterly corrupt. Worse, the authority of the Church was being challenged by kings and emperors like Philip the Fat of France and Henry IV of Germany. It was Henry who had led an army into Rome and forcibly elected his own man, Guibert of Ravenna (Clement III), the false pope.

Outside the Church there were other problems. The barons who ruled the land were constantly fighting with each other. Their raids swept back and forth, often doing more harm to bystanders than to the combatants. Some years earlier the Church had tried to slow the fighting by proclaiming the Truce of God. It promised exile or excommunication for any person who killed or wounded another or made war anytime between Wednesday evening and sunrise the following Monday. The truce had been a failure. It seemed that nothing could stop the feuds and family quarrels that were the root of the bloodshed.

Urban had been considering all these things when he crossed the mountains between Italy and France and called the conference. Even more important was a letter he had received from Alexius Comnenus, the emperor of Byzantium.

Urban saw in that letter an opportunity to solve at one stroke most of the problems that beset him. He could redirect the fighting spirit of the barons, give the Church a new mission, and discredit Guibert at the same time. He had no way of knowing that he was about to unleash one of the greatest armies Europe had ever known. He was about to begin a war that would rage for nearly two hundred years across the places where Christ had walked and preached his message of love and the Kingdom of God. He had no way of knowing that a quite different kingdom would be set up in that place, or that historians would later say of the movement: "It was the last giant step out of the Dark Ages."

Urban and the people who lived then probably would have been surprised to hear their age described as "dark." After all, "dark" is a relative term, and they knew no other way of life than their own. There were undoubtedly men who traveled to the East and, seeing the riches of Constantinople, thought the European castles poor by comparison. The Church had kept alive the memory of Rome, and there were ruins to remind anyone who passed them. But it had been six hundred years since the last Roman emperor in the West surrendered to a barbarian chief named Odoacer. Memories were dim.

It was in 476 that Odoacer stripped the crown from Romulus Augustus, the last emperor. In actual fact, the event was something of an anticlimax. The city of Rome had already been sacked twice—by the Goths in 410 and again by the Vandals in 455. The capital of the western empire had been moved to Ravenna in northern Italy in 402. So the fall of Rome was only the last gasp of an empire already dead.

The *idea* of Rome did not die so easily. It was kept alive partly by the survival of the empire in the East and partly by the spread of Christianity. Both were due in large part to the Roman emperor Constantine.

Constantine is best known as the first Roman emperor to convert to Christianity. But he is also remembered as the founder of the city that bore his name—Constantinople. In 330, Constantine moved from Rome and ordered a new capital built on the western shores of the Bosporus. It was a well-chosen site. The city was surrounded on three sides by water, and protected by a strong army, it was almost impregnable.

Sixty years after Constantine's death, the Roman empire was split, and Rome was soon swallowed by the barbarians. But Constantinople continued to rule over the eastern empire, which came to be known as Byzantium to distinguish it from the old Roman empire.

It was in the West that the invaders managed to erase almost all traces of the former empire. The descendants of Odoacer settled in the countries they overran, but they were soon conquered in turn by fresh waves of invaders. In the eighth and ninth centuries the Vikings, or Norsemen, moved out from Scandinavia in their dragon ships and began raiding coastlines all around Europe. At first they were raids for loot and blood. Their god was a god of war—Odin. To the Norsemen there was no greater glory than death in battle. But eventually even the Norsemen began to settle in the places they had conquered. They married rather than raped the women they found. They were converted to Christianity. They became feudal lords rather than barbarian chiefs. But their descendants never gave up their love for war.

Add to the constant warfare an average life span of about thirty-five years, an infant mortality rate of over 50 percent, and the ever-present danger of plague and famine, and the age can truly be called dark. But life was not total chaos. There were a few bright spots.

One of them was the Church. In the monasteries, one of the most important jobs of the monks was preserving ancient manuscripts. The safeguarding and copying of books which only the clerics could read, and few of *them* could understand, was a work of love. The manuscripts were illuminated in bright colors, pondered over, and hidden in deep vaults whenever danger threatened. A man might spend years copying and illustrating a single book.

The monasteries also served as hospitals, sanctuaries, and roadside stops for anyone brave or foolish enough to travel. Many of those travelers were pilgrims on their way to some shrine as a penance for their sins. Some were on their way to Rome, and a few ventured as far as Jerusalem.

Pilgrimage was an important part of medieval life, even in the darkest days. Almost every town boasted the possession of relics from some saint or one of the apostles. Pieces of the True Cross, on which Christ had been crucified, were scattered through churches all over Europe. People believed genuinely in the power of these relics. A pilgrimage to a famous shrine could absolve them of sin, and miraculous cures were sometimes reported.

For many people, religion was the only thing that made life bearable. The average man worked in fields he did not own from sunrise to sunset, slept in a mud or thatch hut with only scraps of wood for heat, and watched without hope as half his crop was taken away from him by the lord of the manor. He was tied to the land, and he had no legal rights except those established by custom. He could not leave his village or marry without permission. And in some places *droit du seigneur* was still in practice. This was the custom that allowed the lord of the manor to take to his own bed his vassal's newly married bride on her wedding night.

In the face of all this, the only place a man could turn for consolation was the Church. True, the Church promised no immediate revolutionary changes on earth, but the afterlife was a different matter. There, all people were judged equally, and the rewards promised were unimaginable. The idea of heaven, purgatory, and hell was very real.

The Church was also the great unifier. There were no nations as we know them. A man's political loyalty extended no farther than the castle on the hill overlooking his village. The Church had a universal language—Latin—and it had a single supreme leader—the pope. Its organization provided stability in a chaotic world and gave people an identity. Whatever else they might be, they were all Christians.

The Church had grown to a position of great power over the years. The power was not limited to spiritual affairs. Many monasteries owned large tracts of land, and some kept standing armies to defend it. Land was the only wealth, and wealth led the Church inevitably into corruption. In the eleventh century, bishops' offices were routinely bought and sold. Absolution could be bought for the right price. And in 1045 the papacy itself was sold by Benedict IX to a man named John Gratian (Gregory VI), who lasted a year before he too was forced to abdicate. By the end of the eleventh century, however, a spirit of reform was stirring the Church. Urban II was about to prove himself one of the greatest of the reformers.

While the Church ruled the spiritual world, a different system had evolved to rule the temporal. Feudalism was a complex, unwritten code based on ownership of the land. In theory one man—king or emperor—was sole ruler of the land, and he gave the right of usage to other men, called vassals, who ruled under him. The vassals of the king had vassals in turn, until finally the bottom of the pyramid—the serfs—was reached. In return for the right to rule over lands and promises of protection, the vassal offered services—military and civilian—financial aid in wartime, and an oath of loyalty to the man above him, known as his suzerain.

The theory did not always work. In practice, it was the suzerain with the strongest army who commanded the largest lands and the loyalty of his vassals. In some cases a vassal might end up holding lands granted to him by two different suzerains. In case of war between the suzerains (which was not unlikely), the vassal had to decide which side to join. If he was smart or lucky, he joined the winner.

The system has been described by some historians as organized anarchy, and the term fits pretty well. There was no written law, and the nobles ruled with absolute power. A serf could be hanged or have his hands cut off for simple offenses like poaching or cutting wood in the forests. Murder among the nobles was avenged by members of the victim's family, so there were constant feuds.

The nobles were intimidated to some extent by the Church, which held over them the power of excommunication—a fearsome weapon in those days. And they governed themselves by a loose code of chivalry. It was not the chivalry of later times or of legend. It was little more than a series of unwritten qualifications for knighthood.

Physical courage and skill in war were the great virtues. A boy born into a noble family began training for knighthood from the moment he learned to walk. He was taught to ride, wield a sword, build siege engines, and employ elementary tactics. In those days tactics consisted of a frontal charge with the knights. Once the knights were mounted and massed in tight formation, they were unstoppable. Even on foot a knight with his broadsword could take on as many as ten ordinary soldiers.

Knights did not wear the massive armor they would adopt in later years. In the eleventh century, armor was made of iron rings sewn into leather tunics, with gloves and leggings of chain mail. The helmet was a simple iron cap with a long nosepiece. The knight's main protection was his sword. Swords were massive three-foot blades with hilts and pommels of iron. The knights of the Middle Ages swung their swords easily in one hand and carried a heavy, kite-shaped shield in the other.

This, then, was the world Urban was to address—rough, unlettered, and still barbaric. It has been called by many names. It was an age of war, of faith, and of simple cruelty. And as Urban made his way through the crowd and took his place on the platform, it was ready to explode.

The crowd hushed as Urban stood in front of them. He began speaking in their own language, and the people in front passed what they heard to those in back, too far away to hear.

Urban began by speaking of a new danger from the East. A barbaric race of invaders had taken over the holy places in Palestine, and was slaughtering and torturing Christian pilgrims. This same race also threatened the Christian empire of Byzantium. The emperor had sent an appeal for help. But it was Urban's account of the desecration in Jerusalem that really ignited the fury of the crowd.

Urban told them how the invaders were using Christian churches to stable their horses and of the Christian blood that was being poured over altars. Women were raped, and pilgrims were cut open to get at money they had swallowed to protect themselves from robbery.

Then Urban pricked their consciences. He reminded the nobles of the heavy burden of sin they were carrying. They had slain and robbed each other, and forgotten the true service of Christ. There was a way to atone for all this.

"Go out in the defense of Christ," he told the crowd. He called for a war against the invader—a war that would take back the Holy Land and restore the places where Christ had lived to their true protectors.

Urban was a powerful speaker. He promised absolution for the sins of anyone who died in battle or along the way. And carried away by the power of his voice, the promises, and the name of the holy city, Jerusalem, the crowd responded.

Swords rattled in their sheaths and were raised like banners. A shout rose from the crowd, was picked up, and became deafening. It was the shout that would become the battle cry and inspiration of the Crusade:

"God wills it!"

2

the prophet of allah

While Urban made his appeal to the crowd outside Clermont, another call was being heard a thousand miles away in cities and towns all through the East. It was the muezzin's call to prayer. Five times a day it rang out, and millions of the faithful spread their prayer rugs and knelt, facing Mecca, as required by the Koran. Their religion was Islam, which means "submission," and they were known as Muslims, the followers of Muhammad.

It had been almost five hundred years since Muhammad proclaimed his message of the one God to a few skeptical listeners outside his family. Since that time Islam had raced like a fire storm across Arabia and exploded throughout the East, reaching even into Europe.

The explosion began in an improbable place. Arabia had never played an important part in history. At the time of Muhammad's birth, around 570, it was split among a number of warring clans. They were nomads for the most part. Their only interest in the outside world was trade. Their caravans roamed between the trading center of Mecca and the cities of Syria.

Arab religion was pagan; it included the worship of stones, trees, and hundreds of idols. The most sacred of their idols was a

17

small black stone that had fallen from heaven and now rested in Mecca at a place called the Kaaba. By the sixth century, though, Christian missionaries had made a large number of converts. There was a colony of Jews at Medina. New religious ideas were taking hold.

Not much is known about Muhammad's early life. He was an orphan, raised by an uncle who was the leader of his clan. He may have traveled with his uncle over the caravan routes, and he never learned to read and write. Most importantly, he developed an eager interest in religion.

Muhammad studied the religious beliefs of Christians and Jews, and soon came to agree with them on one thing: There could be only one God.

Through most of his life Muhammad kept rigid prayer vigils. He fasted sometimes, and spent time alone in a cave outside the city where he could think and pray without being interrupted. When he was about forty, Muhammad experienced a series of visions and revelations he claimed were sent by God. Over the years he dictated the revelations he received, and these became the Koran, which means "reading" or "recitation."

The substance of Muhammad's religion can be summed up in a single sentence: "There is no God but God [in Arabic, Allah], and Muhammad is his prophet." Not many people in Mecca were willing to accept Muhammad as a prophet, however, and in 622 he traveled to Medina to begin his real missionary work. The journey is known as the hegira, and 622 marks the year 1 on the Muslim calendar.

The simplicity of Islam appealed to many people who were confused by the complicated Christian theology. In Medina, Muhammad was well received by everyone except the Jews, who refused to listen to him. He turned then to the nomads and preached a *jihad*, or holy war ordered by God, against all who would not submit to the new faith. Within two years Muhammad was master over most of Arabia. He died in 632, but his followers carried on the war he had proclaimed against the infidel.

Muhammad's successors were called the caliphs. The first of them, a former merchant named Abu Bakr, began the attack on

Palestine, which was still part of the East Roman (Byzantine) Empire. Abu died in 634, before he really had a chance to get started. It was the second caliph, Omar, who rode to the top of the hills surrounding Jerusalem and prepared a siege.

Omar's siege of Jerusalem lasted a year, but from the beginning there was little hope of relief for the city. The Arab forces rolled up the countryside, cutting Jerusalem off from the sea and preventing Byzantine forces from landing. It is not likely that Constantinople could have come to the rescue in any case. The Byzantine Empire had just finished a long war with the Persians, which had left the armies on both sides drained.

Inside Jerusalem the Christian patriarch, Sophronius, led the defense. It was brave effort, but by the end of a year provisions in the city were running low. The defenders faced starvation. Sophronius rode out to meet Omar and negotiate surrender terms. Sophronius asked that imperial Byzantine officials be given safe conduct to the coast, where they could take ships to Constantinople. The request was granted. For the rest of the city things were not so easy.

Christians and Jews were allowed to live and practice their religion, since Muhammad had proclaimed them People of the Book—those who worshiped one God. For the rest, the choice was conversion to Islam or death. A few chose to die, but many more accepted the new religion.

That choice was the basis of conversion wherever Islam spread. Within ten years Egypt, Persia, and Armenia had fallen, along with Syria and Palestine. The one force that stood between the Muslims and the rest of Europe was the Byzantine army. With its outer provinces lost, Byzantine resistance stiffened. Muslims attacked Constantinople by sea, but were turned back with heavy losses. Most of the Muslim ships were lost to the Byzantine secret weapon, Greek fire. It was a terrible weapon, shot out of tubes from ships or city walls, much like a modern flamethrower. The fire burned on water, so it was impossible to put it out.

In the south the Muslims did better. Their armies spread across North Africa, took Sicily, and in 711 invaded Spain. They might have gone farther, but in 732 a Frankish king known as Charles the

Hammer met a Muslim force near Tours in France and defeated them. The Muslims retreated from France and did not try to cross the Pyrenees Mountains again.

After Charles's victory the Muslim expansion was over. It was not so much the Franks who had stopped them as it was the old story of internal squabbles. They had simply run out of gas.

When the conquests ended, the Muslims ruled an empire that stretched from the Indus River to the Spanish shores of the Atlantic. Converts were soon being made as far away as the borders of China and Malaya.

Once the first shock was over, the Christians and Jews in the conquered countries discovered that their new masters were no more oppressive than the old ones. In some cases the people were better off than they had been under the Byzantines. This was particularly true with the Syrian and Egyptian Christians, who had been persecuted as heretics because of their differences with the Eastern Church.

In addition, the taxes the Muslims imposed on their Christian subjects were lower than taxes had been under the Byzantines. Christians and Jews could not carry weapons or ride horses, but that was not a special hardship. They were not allowed to build new churches or synagogues or to make converts among the Muslims. But the religious buildings that stood were respected.

So, in general, life went on in the conquered countries much as it had before. Over the years many of the children born into Christian families accepted Islam. The sight of the mosques and the sound of the muezzin became a familiar fact of life in Jerusalem.

Pilgrims from the West were welcomed in Jerusalem. Part of the reason, of course, was the money they brought. Inns were set up for pilgrims in the Holy City, and guides showed them to all the important shrines. A brisk business in rather dubious relics was set up.

Hospitality to pilgrims was also a diplomatic gesture. Travelers usually stopped first in Constantinople, and from there many took ships to the eastern Mediterranean cities of Tyre in Phoenicia (Lebanon) and Caesarea in Palestine (south of Haifa, Israel). In the tenth century the Byzantines had managed to recapture some of their losses, including the city of Antioch (Antakya, in southern Turkey). But through most of the eleventh, Byzantine and Arab were at peace with each other. The pilgrim's journey, once he reached Byzantine territory, was not terribly dangerous.

The Arab world, like the Christian, had split on religious questions shortly after Muhammad's death. Two sects, the Shiites and the Sunnites, had grown up. By the eleventh century there had been a serious political division as well. There were now caliphs ruling in Cairo, Baghdad, Damascus, and even in far-off Córdova, Spain. They were all bitterly opposed. The day of the united Arab front was over.

The Byzantines looked on the split with relief. It gave them breathing space. Constantinople had fought off one enemy after another for seven hundred years. The empire was exhausted. Under the Muslim assault it had shrunk until all that was left was Greece, Asia Minor, and a portion of Italy. The breathing space was short-lived. In 1040 the Byzantines were confronted by a new enemy from the West.

The descendants of the Norsemen had settled in northern France, in a region now known as Normandy. They were restless people still, always looking for new lands to conquer. Soon England would fall to them, but for now they had their eyes on a richer prize—the Byzantine provinces in Italy.

In 1040, six brothers, the sons of a Norman knight named Tancred, began attacking southern Italy. The pope in Rome tried to stop them, but his small army was easily routed. The next pope, terrified lest the Normans decided to take Rome as well, recognized the conquests as legal. By 1060 all the Byzantine possessions in Italy except a single fortress on the coast had fallen. Shortly after, the Normans landed in Sicily and drove the Arabs from the island. It was a sign of things to come.

The invasion was the beginning of a long period of hatred between Constantinople and the Normans. The Normans considered the Byzantines weak, effeminate cowards, which was not entirely just. No race of cowards could have survived seven hundred years of almost constant warfare. On the other hand, the Byzantines thought the Normans were little better than barbarians and murderers. Aside from the mutual hatred, the invasions had a more lasting effect on the attitudes of the Latin and Byzantine churches. The division between them, which had never been very deep, was suddenly widened. The split would have tragic consequences later on.

But the Byzantines were soon distracted from their quarrel with the Normans by a new threat. This time it came from a familiar direction.

The Seljuk Turks were nomads from the steppes of central Asia. They were fairly recent converts to Islam, but they had not had time to acquire an appreciation of Arab civilization. Like the Normans, they were only interested in new territories to conquer. By 1055 they had deposed the caliph and were ruling in Baghdad. Soon they were raiding eastern Byzantine outposts.

For the next twenty years the Turks picked away at the Byzantines, conquering one city after another. The once powerful Byzantine army had fallen apart, and there was little that could be done to stop the Turks. Finally in 1071 the Emperor Romanus scraped together an army mostly composed of mercenaries and marched on the Turks in Armenia, the eastern frontier.

About half of Romanus' mercenary force was composed of Normans under a knight called Roussel. The other half was made up of men who were distant relatives of the Seljuks, the Kuman Turks. With allies like these, Romanus never had a chance.

Romanus was badly outnumbered, and he soon proved himself incompetent as a general as well. First he split his forces, sending the mercenaries ahead to capture a fortress on the shores of Lake Van. With the remainder of his army he marched toward a place called Manzikert (Malazgirt).

The Battle of Manzikert has been called one of the most important battles in the history of the East. It was certainly one of the greatest disasters in the history of the Byzantine Empire.

When Romanus learned that the main body of the Turks was approaching him, he turned to try to join the two halves of his army. On Friday, August 19, 1071, Romanus entered a valley without sending out scouts. The Seljuks were waiting.

Romanus fought well, trying to hold out until his mercenaries could come to his rescue. It was not until later, with his army destroyed and himself wounded and taken prisoner, that he learned the Kumans had decided to join the enemy. The Normans had simply decided to go home. They had not been paid in months.

With the Byzantine army destroyed, all Asia Minor lay open to the Turks. The Byzantines never recovered from Manzikert. Over the next several years they had to fight Normans under Roussel—who saw a chance to set up a kingdom for himself—put down revolts in several provinces, and watch the Turks advance through Asia Minor.

The Turks might have gone on to Constantinople itself if it had not been for two things. First, they continually had to stop to settle civil wars as one leader after another tried to take power. And second, they were foiled by a remarkable emperor who took over the Byzantine throne in 1081. His name was Alexius Comnenus.

Alexius was not a great fighter, but he was a brilliant diplomat. For years Alexius used bribes, alliances, and false promises to play one Turkish chief off against another. When he had to, he led his armies into the field, but he always avoided the type of showdown that had led to disaster at Manzikert. The Turkish invasion never reached Constantinople. The closest they came was Nicaea (Iznik), a city several miles to the southeast.

While the Turks were harassing the Byzantines, they were also making things difficult for native Christians and pilgrims in Palestine. The Turks were not as tolerant as the Arabs had been; they had not been living side by side with "infidels" for three centuries. Stories of atrocities began filtering into the towns and villages of the West.

Alexius was aware of the atrocity stories, and they may have figured in his calculations. After fourteen years his game with the Turks was beginning to pay off. The Turks were spent, fighting among themselves, and, for the moment, not a serious threat to Constantinople. Alexius decided the time had come to counterattack.

He sat down to write a letter to the Western pope.

3

the people's crusade

Alexius had hoped for nothing more than a few hundred mercenaries. He had not counted on Urban's call for a Crusade. He would have been shocked at the rattle of swords and the sight of the shouting, weeping crowd, which cried with one voice: "God wills it!"

But for Urban, standing on the platform in the midst of the milling throng, the shout was a sign. He raised his hand for silence. "God has drawn these words from you," he told the crowd. "Let this be your battle cry. When an attack is made upon the enemy, let this one cry be raised by all the soldiers of God: 'God wills it!' "

Among the men with Urban on the platform was Adhemar, the bishop of Le Puy. Adhemar hurried to where the pope stood and dropped on one knee in front of him. He begged permission to go with the army. Urban not only granted permission, but appointed Adhemar as his personal representative and spiritual commander of the army. Hundreds of others hastened forward to follow Adhemar's example.

Urban continued to talk, laying down rules for the assembly and conduct of the army. The old, the sick, and those unfit to bear

24

arms were ordered to stay home. Women could go only if they were accompanied by their husbands or guardians. The rich should aid the needy. The Truce of God should be observed, and everyone who went should sew on his clothing strips of cloth in the shape of a cross to identify him as a member of God's army.

The meeting broke up, but Urban stayed at Clermont for five more days. He was gladdened by the response, but he knew the real test was yet to come. Perhaps two or three thousand people had heard the speech. None of the important nobility, who would provide the real strength of the army if there was to be one, had been there. Then, on December 1, messengers sent by Count Raymond of Toulouse arrived at Clermont. Raymond and most of his knights were ready to take the cross. Urban left Clermont the next day, confident the Crusade was off to a good start.

For the rest of the winter and through spring, Urban traveled through France, gathering support and preaching holy war. The word went out from hundreds of pulpits and monasteries. On every tongue the one topic was Jerusalem. One by one the nobles, great and small, joined the throng.

After Raymond came a surprise. Hugh of Vermandois, brother of Philip the Fat, had taken the cross. Philip had been excommunicated for adultery—which was probably the least of his crimes—and was famous for the gross debauchery of his court. Carried away by enthusiasm for the movement, Philip wrote to Urban, offering his submission to the pope and informing him of Hugh's decision.

Even the vassals of Henry IV were coming. The most important was Godfrey of Bouillon, with his brothers Eustace and Baldwin. In Normandy, Duke Robert and his brother-in-law, Stephen of Blois, began assembling a company of knights for the march to Jerusalem. And in Italy, a Norman prince who had once fought alongside the Norman invaders of Byzantium took up the cross. His name was Bohemond of Taranto. If Alexius had known Bohemond and his nephew Tancred were coming, he might not have written his letter. Alexius had good reason to fear them. They had not forgotten their ambition to carve off pieces of the Byzantine Empire.

All through the spring and summer of 1096 the gathering

swelled like a tide. The combined armies grew so large that the chroniclers of the time gave up any hope of counting them. They compared their numbers to "grains of sand along the beach." In villages and hamlets all across Europe, fires burned in forges as smiths hammered out new weapons—swords, pikes, and thousands of arrows. And each day some new knight rode up to his lord's castle to take the strips of cloth and sew them to his tunic.

Urban had set the date for departure as August 15, 1096, and instructed the armies to meet at Constantinople. But there were some who grew impatient. They were led by a strange little man who rode a donkey through the forests and fields of France and the Rhineland, gathering followers and preaching a vision of Jerusalem. His name was Peter the Hermit.

Peter made his first appearance shortly after Urban's speech at Clermont. At one time he may have been a monk, but in 1095 he made a poor living as a traveling preacher. He was clothed in rags, and even in an age not noted for baths he was remarkable for the filthiness of his dress. No one knew much about him, but all who met him agreed he was a holy man.

Peter made an extraordinary impact on the people of northern France. Great crowds followed him wherever he went. Many people plucked hairs from his donkey, cherishing the prizes as holy relics. Most of Peter's followers were the poor. There were old people, serfs who had left their fields lying fallow, women and children. There were townsmen, thieves, prostitutes, and beggars from the gutters of Paris. They were simple, unlettered, and they believed implicitly in the man who rode in front of them. Even the nobles were impressed by Peter. None had any desire to join him, but many gave him money, which he immediately distributed among his followers.

By March 1096, Peter's band had swelled to nearly 15,000 people. They turned northward in that month toward Cologne, where Peter planned to stop for a while and gather more men. As they marched, people would come running from the towns they passed and ask, "Where are you going?"

The answer was always the same: "Jerusalem."

Hardly any of them knew where Jerusalem was, but they knew

what they would find when they got there. It was God's city. It was not a city in Palestine they were thinking of. The heavenly Jerusalem was all they knew. Most of them believed they were setting out to find it. They were poorly armed, undisciplined, and totally incapable of standing up to any Turkish army. But they believed in miracles.

Of course not all of Peter's followers were moved by a vision of Jerusalem. There was a fair number of adventurers and camp followers anxious to pick up any loot that might fall their way. It is a credit to Peter's ability to lead people that he was able to keep this mob together.

There was one renowned knight who traveled with Peter, known as Walter-sans-Avoir—Walter the Penniless. He had earned his name by giving all his possessions to the poor before the Crusade started. All the witnesses of the time describe him as a man of courage and bearing. With Walter there were eight other knights and a few hundred foot soldiers. They were the only strength in Peter's army.

Peter decided to stay in Cologne during April, but Walter was anxious to push on. So while Peter preached in Cologne, Walter and a few thousand others crossed the Rhine and followed the Danube into Hungary. Hungary was a Christian country, so the Crusaders expected little trouble. Walter sent messages to Koloman, the Hungarian king, asking permission to pass through the country and for provisions for his followers. Koloman was helpful, and by the end of the first week in May, Walter reached Belgrade.

But before the arrival in Belgrade, an unfortunate incident occurred that would have repercussions later on. In a town called Maleville (perhaps Zemun in Yugoslavia; *maleville*, which means, roughly, "evil city," may have been only the name given the town by the Franks) sixteen of Walter's men got into an argument with some merchants. The Crusaders naturally blamed the townsmen for the quarrel, claiming they had been cheated over some purchase. It is more likely that the sixteen were caught stealing. In any case, they were stripped, their arms were taken from them, and they were turned out of the city. Their arms were hung on the city walls as a warning to future thieves. The men were not harmed, and Walter did not learn of the incident until it was too late to do anything about it.

Belgrade was the western outpost of the Byzantine Empire, and Walter expected to be welcomed. But the governor had not received any word from Constantinople about a crusading army from the West. He was not prepared for them. The harvest had not been gathered, and there was little food available. While the governor waited for instructions from the capital, some of Walter's men began raiding the countryside, stealing food wherever they could find it. The commander of the Byzantine province was enraged.

A Byzantine force cut off one of the foraging parties, and fighting broke out. Walter's men were scattered. Some attempted to barricade themselves inside a church. The Byzantines burned the church to the ground, and sixty men died inside. Walter escaped with most of his forces to Nish (Nis), a city south of Belgrade. There, word had come from Alexius, and peace was restored. The governor at Nish gave Walter arms and money to continue his journey. By the middle of July, Walter finally arrived at Constantinople.

Peter was not far behind. He had left Cologne on April 20 with about 20,000 people. They followed Walter's route, and all was well until they reached Maleville. When they saw the arms hanging from the city wall, they naturally assumed that the men had been murdered by the townspeople. The Crusaders attacked the city. The surprised Hungarians had no chance. The fighting raged most of the day. Thousands of Hungarian Christians were slaughtered, and the town was looted.

Peter might have gotten away with the massacre, but he stayed in Maleville for five days, gathering provisions and stripping the town. It gave the Hungarians time to retaliate. King Koloman heard of the slaughter and sent a small army after Peter. While Peter's men were crossing a river, the Hungarians attacked with showers of arrows. In the confusion, several boats were swamped. Dozens of Peter's men were drowned. The Crusaders managed to beat off the smaller Hungarian force and executed seven captives.

After the incident at Maleville, Peter made it to Constantinople without further trouble. But he had made sure that any Crusaders who followed would not be welcome in the Danube region.

As badly as Peter's followers sometimes behaved, they were saints compared to some other groups who started out from Germany. Among them was a certain Emich of Leisingen, a bandit, soldier, and murderer who claimed to have had a cross miraculously branded into the hair on his chest by God. Emich collected a large following, but rather than take Peter's road to the East, Emich decided to attack what he considered some enemies of Christ closer to home.

Colonies of Jews had been living peacefully in towns in Germany and France for centuries. Many of them were traders and merchants, keeping contacts with other Jews in Byzantium. They were an important source of economic strength. Some acted as moneylenders, since the Christian Church prohibited its members from charging interest on loans—a practice they called usury—and others were doctors. Since they were important people, the Jews were usually protected by the Church and the nobles who ruled the towns.

But by the end of the eleventh century, things were beginning to change. Anti-Jewish feeling had been smoldering, and with the preaching of the Crusade it burst into the open. Emich's mob, and bands led by two other men named Volkmar and Gottschalk, turned on the Jews in a number of German cities. Their reasons were partly religious, partly resentment directed against people who were generally better off than they themselves were. And of course there was the opportunity to pick up more loot.

The first attack came in the town of Spier (Speyer). The bishop of the town placed the Jews under his protection, but about twelve Jews were murdered by Emich's mob. The bishop saved the rest and caught some of the killers. He ordered that those caught have their hands cut off as punishment and a warning to others. But the bishop's action did not deter Emich.

On May 20, Emich massacred five hundred Jews at Worms, and five days later he reached the city of Mainz. The archbishop of Mainz had closed the gates, but on May 26 riots broke out inside the city. Someone threw open the gates, and Emich marched on the archbishop's palace, where the Jews were gathered. There was a brief sharp fight, and then Emich set fire to the palace. The bishop and most of the palace defenders were driven out.

Inside a great hall, the Jews of the city listened as Emich's men battered at the door. The hinges gave way, and the mob surged into the hall. There was one Christian knight who tried to defend the people he was guarding, but he was quickly overwhelmed. With swords and axes, Emich's men began the slaughter.

The Jews were helpless, and Emich spared no one, not men, women, or children. With the courage of despair, the Jewish men pulled out short knives and began killing their wives and children—quickly, mercifully. Then they turned their weapons on themselves. A thousand people died that day.

After Worms, Emich turned to Cologne, but there he was stopped. The Christians of the city had hidden the Jews in their homes, and Emich was able to capture only two men. They were killed when they refused to convert to Christianity. Emich burned a synagogue and finally set out to the East.

Meanwhile Volkmar and Gottschalk were attacking Jewish settlements in the East. In Prague, Jews were massacred by Volkmar, and a similar massacre took place in Ratisbon (Regensburg) in Bavaria under Gottschalk's direction.

The Hungarians were in no mood, after the trouble with Walter and Peter, for patience with Crusaders. When Gottschalk's men entered Hungary, the Hungarian army fell on them. The Crusaders were wiped out to the last man. A few days later the same fate befell Volkmar.

By the time Emich reached Hungary, King Koloman was waiting. He refused permission to cross the border, and fortified a bridge Emich's men would have to use to cross the Danube. Fighting broke out instantly.

For six weeks Emich attacked the bridge while some of his men constructed another bridge a short way downriver. Finally they forced their way across.

Koloman's army fell back to the city of Wieselburg on the Hungarian side of the river. The city walls stopped the attackers momentarily. But among Emich's men were some who were experienced in siege warfare. They built engines—massive batter-

ing rams, catapults, and towers—and began undermining the
walls. With the engines and mines they tore huge holes in the
walls, and the assault broke through. It looked like another massacre would take place.

But then something happened—one of those unexplained oc-
currences which many chroniclers called a miracle. At the very
moment when victory seemed certain, a strange panic gripped
Emich's men. They surged into the city with the Hungarians
retreating before them—and stopped.

The Hungarians had set fire to parts of the city to keep it from
falling into Emich's hands. Perhaps it was the smoke and flame.
Perhaps Emich saw something. Whatever it was, the Crusaders
suddenly turned and fled, with no one pursuing them.

The Hungarian army, seeing the panic in Emich's ranks, re-
grouped. They charged into the Crusader camp, cutting down the
fleeing men on all sides. Very few escaped. Among those who
managed to get away was Emich. He returned to Germany, his
crusade ended. The people who listened to his story shuddered. It
seemed to them that the defeat was a sign of God's displeasure.
"So the hand of God was against the pilgrims," Albert of Aix
wrote, "who had slaughtered the Jews through greed of money."

Many people wondered. The cry of "God wills it!" sounded
suddenly very hollow.

4

the barons set out

The summer was waning, and the barons were on the march.
From Normandy, from southern France and Italy, and from
Lorraine the armies ran like rivers toward their meeting place—
the Bosporus and Constantinople.

The first to set out was Hugh of Vermandois. He left late in
August with a small company of knights and foot soldiers and
headed toward Italy. He planned to take the sea route across the
Adriatic and travel through the northern parts of Greece to Constantinople. Before leaving, he sent a messenger ahead to inform
Alexius that he was coming. "Know, O King," Hugh wrote, "that
I am King of Kings and superior to all who are under the sky. You
are now permitted to greet me on my arrival, and to receive me
with magnificence as befits my nobility."

This astonishing bit of arrogance was greeted with howls of
laughter at the Byzantine court. Hugh's dignity was merely
pricked by the laughter; it was completely demolished by the
manner of his arrival. He was shipwrecked off the coast of Greece
and forced to save himself in a small boat, which was washed up
on the shore. Soaked, shivering with cold, and with most of his
men lost, he was met by two servants of the Byzantine governor.

Hugh was given a horse and was treated well by his hosts. After a few days he was sent on with a Byzantine escort to Constantinople. He was impressed by the size of his protective escort, and pleased that so much attention was being paid to him. He didn't know it yet, but he was virtually a prisoner.

As funny as Hugh's note had seemed, Alexius saw he was going to have trouble with the Crusaders. His greatest fear was that the armies from the West would unite and turn on Constantinople. It was not an unreasonable suspicion, especially with men like Bohemond. So Alexius had devised a plan.

Hugh was treated to a shower of gifts from Alexius. He was received in the palace with all the honor he had demanded and more. He was dazzled by the richness of the city and the size of the banquets spread before him. He was even more dazzled by the man who could afford to pour out such wealth. So when Alexius asked Hugh to swear an oath of loyalty, as was the Western custom, Hugh agreed.

The oath was serious, since it made Hugh the vassal of Alexius. It required Hugh to turn over to Alexius any former Byzantine cities that were recaptured from the Turks. It was not an oath Hugh could or would readily break. It was part of Alexius' plan to extract such a promise from each of the leaders of the Crusade. He did not find it so easy with the next arrival, Godfrey of Bouillon.

Godfrey was about thirty-five at the time, tall and built with the solid frame of a true knight. He was a second son, and most of his father's wealth and lands had fallen to his older brother, Eustace, when their father died. Godfrey's inheritance had come from an uncle in Lower Lorraine. He was not too attached to the lands he had received. He gave them up easily enough when he heard the call for a Crusade.

Godfrey's younger brother, Baldwin, had even less to lose when he took the cross. As a third son he was destined for the Church, but he had quickly decided that was not the life for him. When he set out on the Crusade, he had no intention of returning home. He meant to set up a kingdom for himself or die in the attempt.

Godfrey and Baldwin had followed Peter the Hermit's route through Hungary without trouble. It was not a rabble that Godfrey led, but a strong, well-disciplined army. King Koloman wisely recognized the difference. He gave Godfrey permission to cross Hungary, and only asked that Baldwin remain with the Hungarians as a hostage to ensure the Crusaders' good behavior. Godfrey kept a tight rein on his army. Baldwin was returned safely when they reached Bulgaria.

With the usual Byzantine escort keeping watch, Godfrey arrived at Constantinople two days before Christmas, 1096. The man sent by Alexius to meet him was Hugh of Vermandois. Godfrey had heard of Hugh's capture and was surprised to see him so well fed and apparently contented. Hugh urged Godfrey to take the oath as he had done. Godfrey refused. He was suspicious and a little contemptuous of the French count who had surrendered so meekly.

When Hugh brought back Godfrey's refusal, Alexius applied a little pressure. He cut off all supplies to Godfrey's camp. Godfrey didn't want to provoke open warfare, but Baldwin was more impetuous. With a few knights he began raiding the outskirts of the city. Alexius hastily lifted the blockade.

For three months there was a stalemate. The winter rains turned Godfrey's camp into a quagmire, and Alexius offered to move him to the suburbs across the inlet known as the Golden Horn. Godfrey agreed to the move.

Alexius was not really concerned with Godfrey's comfort. The move took the Crusaders away from the city and made it easier for the Byzantine army to keep an eye on them. The Crusaders resented the guards, and predictably there was soon trouble. Armed clashes broke out. Godfrey seethed in his camp, and then, near the end of March, his temper snapped. Alexius had cut off his supplies again.

Alexius was desperate. Messengers from his western borders had reached him with word that another Crusader army was crossing Greece. At their head was Bohemond of Taranto. Alexius knew that he would have to step up the pressure before the two Crusader forces could join and turn against him.

Once again Baldwin retaliated by raiding the suburbs. Alexius sent a small force of police to stop him, but Baldwin easily routed them.

Godfrey, too, had decided to act. He burned the buildings around his camp and moved back across the Golden Horn. He began an attack on the main city wall. It was a foolish gesture.

Alexius chose not to annihilate Godfrey's men. As troublesome as they were, Alexius knew they would be useful later on. It was only Godfrey's stubborn pride that had to be overcome. Alexius ordered the archers defending the city walls to aim at the Crusader horses and not the men.

Godfrey would not take the hint. With his horses slaughtered, he pressed the attack on foot. Alexius was forced to bring out his full might. After a short skirmish, Godfrey's men were thrown back. Once again Hugh of Vermandois was sent as an ambassador.

"We should not have left our own lands," Hugh said sadly. "But now that we are here, our business will not turn out well unless we give in to the demands of the one who rules here." It was a cringing remark, but it also contained a reminder—that they were being held up from their true business, which was the capture of Jerusalem. By then Godfrey was thoroughly sick of the conflict. He swallowed his pride and agreed to give the oath to Alexius.

Alexius happily gave the same presents to Godfrey that he had showered on Hugh. Then Godfrey and his men were ferried across the Bosporus. He was no sooner gone than scouts reported the arrival of Bohemond.

To Alexius' surprise, Bohemond was perfectly friendly. He made no trouble crossing Byzantine lands, and he took the oath without a murmur. Bohemond may have hated the Byzantines, but he was smart enough to realize the Crusade had no chance of success without their help. And he knew he could not defeat the Byzantine army alone. As for the oath, that was mere words.

Despite Bohemond's friendly attitude, Alexius knew better than to trust him. Both men made a great show of friendship, with presents from Alexius, and an offer of alliance from Bohemond which the emperor quietly ignored. Once Bohemond suggested that he take charge of the combined Byzantine and Crusader armies. The emperor smiled and changed the subject.

"Such a man was Bohemond," Alexius' daughter Anna wrote

years later, remembering the encounter. "Never have I seen anyone so dishonest. . . . He was always first in line whenever money or presents were offered."

As soon as he could decently manage it, Alexius had Bohemond and his men hustled across the strait.

On the day Bohemond was sent across, the third army under Raymond of Toulouse arrived. Raymond was one of the few leaders who came out of genuine religious motives. He was the ruler of a large domain in southern France, where he lived a rich, comfortable life with his wife and children. He was nearly sixty years old, his hair and beard were mottled with gray, and he had already done his fighting against the Muslims in Spain. He saw in the Crusade a last chance for glory as well as an opportunity to serve a cause he believed in. His only complaint was that he had not been appointed the leader of the Crusade.

When he took the cross, Raymond left his lands and his title to his oldest son and swore an oath to die in Palestine. He raised money by selling all his personal possessions, and he took responsibility for a large group of pilgrims who made the journey with him. Among them were his wife and youngest children.

Alexius was impressed with Raymond. He liked him almost at first sight. He did not apply pressure for the oath, as he had with Godfrey. Perhaps Alexius knew it would have been useless. Raymond declared that he had only one master—Christ—and would serve no other. He was the only leader Alexius could not overcome either by force or persuasion. Raymond made only one concession. He promised to respect the life and honor of the emperor.

The last of the armies to arrive was that of Robert of Normandy. It was typical of the short Norman duke that he should be last. It was his usual position in everything he ever attempted.

Robert Curthose they called him—Short Britches would be a roughly modern equivalent. The name had been given to him by his father, William the Conqueror. All his life Robert had been the target of jokes. His main interests in life were wine first and women second. He was incurably lazy, slow to anger, and his good nature allowed him to be tricked by his younger brother, William the Red (William Rufus) of England. But once aroused, Robert was a terrible fighter.

Robert had been given Normandy for an inheritance when their father died, and William was constantly scheming to get it for himself. When word of the Crusade reached Normandy, William saw an opportunity.

Robert was intrigued by the idea of the Crusade, but he had a problem. As usual, he was broke. He worried about it for a few days, and then William came up with a generous offer. He would finance the army, he told Robert, and hold Normandy for him until his return. If Robert did not return within three years and repay the loan, Normandy would become William's.

The idea seemed perfectly fair to Robert. William nearly went bankrupt and taxed his own country to the breaking point in a scramble to gather the needed money. Robert suddenly found himself at the head of a great army as the barons of Normandy joined him.

Among Robert's followers was Count Stephen of Blois. Stephen was probably the most reluctant of all the men who set out on the Crusade. He had just been married to Robert's sister Adele, a woman he loved, and he saw no reason to give up his easy life to pursue infidels. But Adele was also a Norman, a daughter of William the Conqueror, and she had inherited her father's strong will. She could not bear the thought that she might have married a coward.

Robert and Stephen reached Rome in September 1096. They were accompanied by the last great leader of the crusade, Robert of Flanders. Robert is another who seems to have gone crusading from religious motives, although he did not make a great noise about it. He was quiet, dependable, and utterly fearless. The armies of the three men stayed in Rome, visiting St. Peter's and the papal court, then reached the Italian coast in late fall. There they spent the winter. As usual, Robert of Normandy was in no hurry.

Robert finally reached Constantinople in May 1097. He was overwhelmed by riches, just as Hugh had been. He and Stephen gave the required oath willingly. Alexius could breathe easier. With Robert ferried across the strait, the last of the Crusaders had passed.

When Robert reached the eastern shore, he found that the rest of the crusading army had left. They had marched south nearly a month before, to a former Byzantine city called Nicaea. The city had been in the hands of the Turks for ten years. Robert hastened to join the siege, but along the way he had to pass a deserted camp at a place called Cibotus (Civetot). There he saw something that must have shocked him. And he heard from a few wretched stragglers a horrible tale.

Peter the Hermit and his unruly mob had reached Constantinople almost ten months before, on August 1, 1096. The number of his followers had shrunk to about 10,000 people. Most of them were still peasants, women, and children, but a few hundred knights had joined him and several thousand foot soldiers.

Alexius met Peter privately after seeing his army. Alexius was not impressed by the sight. He had some good advice for Peter— not to engage the Turks until he could be joined by the main Crusader army. Peter agreed, but he was fast losing his grip on the mob. They were incurable thieves, and after a week of pillaging, Alexius sent them across the strait.

For a month they camped at Cibotus, about thirty miles north of Nicaea. At the end of that time they were so restless Peter could not restrain them any longer. The mob split into two groups, and the Germans elected a man named Rainauld to lead them. The French followed a man named Geoffrey Burel. In despair, Peter abandoned them and went back to Constantinople.

About the middle of September, Burel led a detachment of men as far as Nicaea, burning villages and looting the countryside. He slaughtered hundreds of people—most of them Greek Christians. The Germans, seeing the loot that was brought back, decided to do a little raiding of their own.

Six thousand men set out near the end of September, passing Nicaea and proceeding until they reached a Turkish fortress at Xerigordon, several miles east of Nicaea. They captured it without much difficulty, but the Turkish sultan at Nicaea, Kilij Arslan, struck back. Thousands of Turks swept down on the fortress, surrounding it and bottling up the Crusaders inside.

The water supply for the fortress came from a spring outside the walls. The Turks cut it off. Under the hot desert sun, the besieged Crusaders grew desperate. For eight days they held out, drinking blood from their horses, sucking dew from stones and the earth, and licking the sweat from their own bodies. On the eighth day Rainauld surrendered. The Turkish terms were brutal. Everyone who renounced Christianity was allowed to live and was carried off into captivity. All the rest were massacred.

The news of the massacre struck Peter's camp like a thunderbolt. The only responsible leader left in the camp was Walter the Penniless. Most of the Crusaders wanted to set out to avenge the slaughter, but Walter wanted to wait until Peter returned from Constantinople—perhaps with help from the emperor. Before Peter returned, there was more news. Kilij Arslan was coming toward the Crusader camp with his army. Over Walter's protests, Geoffrey Burel insisted they go out to meet the attack.

At dawn on October 21, every available man set out on the road to Nicaea. Left behind were the sick, the old men, the women, and the children. The Crusaders had marched barely three miles when they fell into a Turkish ambush.

The battle was a rout. Walter and a few knights stood firm while the battle swirled around them. The rest, stricken with panic, broke and ran toward the camp. The Turks rode them down mercilessly. Walter fell with seven arrows in him.

Within minutes the remnants of the Crusader force reached the camp. The Turkish cavalry was close behind. There was no time to set up any defense. The Turks rode through the tents where many people were still sleeping. Old men and women came out blinking at the light and the noise and were cut down before they knew what was happening. The screams, the sound of plunging horses, and the clash of steel added to the panic. One priest was killed as he said morning Mass at a makeshift altar. Small children were trampled by men and horses.

In the confusion a few hundred people escaped to a nearby fortress. The gates were missing, and there was no roof over the ruins, but with shields, rocks, and timbers they managed to set up a hasty barricade. Behind it they held off the Turkish assault. They were aided when a fire set by the Turks to burn them out turned, and, whipped by the wind, drove the Turks back. All the rest—nearly 15,000 people—were killed that morning. Only a few young girls were spared to be sold in the slave markets of Baghdad and Damascus.

Alexius heard of the massacre and sent men to take out the survivors in the fortress. The Turks left the field and headed back to Nicaea with only a few men lost.

There were too many dead to bury. The bodies were piled up and left lying in the open. Years later Alexius' daughter Anna wrote, describing the scene:

> So great a multitude of Gauls and Normans were cut down that when the bodies of the killed were brought together they made a great mound, lofty as a mountain. Later some barbarians used the bones of the slain in making a wall. It stands to this day, an enclosure of walls built with mixed rocks and bones. . . .

5

dorylaeum

After the massacre at Cibotus, the Turks were supremely confident. They had met the invaders from the West and found them as easy to cut down as wheat in the harvest. They joked about it as they rode their short, swift ponies back to Nicaea. They were laden with loot from Peter's camp. The captives, tied together and stumbling to keep up through the choking dust, would bring a good price.

Kilij Arslan shared his men's contempt for the Franks. His mind was already occupied with a much more formidable enemy several hundred miles to the east. Before the unexpected arrival of Peter's army, Kilij Arslan had been preparing an expedition against the Turkish emir of Danisment, who had been stirring up revolts in Armenia. Civil wars of one kind or another were a way of life with the Turks. So with most of his army Kilij Arslan left Nicaea and marched eastward in the early part of 1097 to take on his enemy. He left behind his wife and children, the royal treasury, and a small garrison of soldiers to defend his capital. He had nothing to worry about. The walls of Nicaea were impregnable.

The sultan was still engaged in his wars in the east when Godfrey of Bouillon and Hugh of Vermandois pitched their camp on the east side of the Bosporus. They were soon joined by Bohemond and Alexius, who brought along a large detachment of his own men. Alexius had no intention of joining the Crusader army. But he offered troops and a Greek general named Manuel Butumites to lead them.

Alexius knew that the road to Jerusalem led through lands that were occupied by Turks—lands that had once been Byzantine. The Crusaders would have to reduce the cities along the road one by one, since they didn't dare leave any Turks to attack their rear. And once the cities were taken, they would have to be turned over to Alexius because of the oath. Sending his own men along would not only give the Crusaders a better chance of success; it would also help to remind them of the oath in case any of them—especially Bohemond—were tempted to forget.

On April 26, 1097, the combined armies struck camp. They loaded tents and supplies onto pack animals, mounted their horses, and set out in a long line toward Nicaea. They reached the city on May 6.

Kilij Arslan was right about the walls. They were more than four miles around and topped by 240 towers. The western side of the city jutted out into a large lake, with the walls rising straight up from the water. The other sides were protected by a moat and an outer wall, smaller than the main one. The outer wall rose twelve feet and was reinforced with towers of its own. From the towers, archers could cover every foot of ground outside the city with a crossfire.

Godfrey and Hugh set up their camp on the north side, and Bohemond placed his near the east wall for the siege to come. The south was reserved for Raymond of Toulouse, who was still several days behind. The Byzantines began setting up their siege engines.

During the first ten days of the siege, messengers from the city passed easily through the holes in the Crusader lines. The lake side of the city was also open, and supplies were carried by boat to the waterside gate. At first the Crusaders could do nothing to stop the traffic on the lake.

When Kilij Arslan heard of the new army setting out toward Nicaea, he became alarmed. He sent an advance guard back to reinforce the city. He promised to return himself as soon as he settled matters with the Danisment emir.

The sultan's advance guard reached Nicaea on the same day as Raymond of Toulouse, May 16. Raymond's tents had not even been pitched in front of the south wall when a line of Turkish horsemen appeared on the hills above the city. The Turks rode toward the south gate. They had been told by spies that it was open. They intended to break through the Crusader lines and join the garrison inside.

There was a brief scramble for weapons and horses among Raymond's men. Then several hundred knights rode out on line. The Turks kept coming—carelessly. They remembered Peter's men.

"God wills it!" The battle cry went up in a roar. The knights charged.

The astonished Turks faltered. They had never seen anything like this. The line of knights rolled into them, swords flashing, their heavier chargers bowling over the Turkish horses. Within moments it was over. The few Turks who survived the first charge turned and scattered for the hills, the Crusaders in pursuit.

Raymond's men rode back happily. This was the kind of fight they liked. They cut off the heads of the Turkish dead and cheerily catapulted them over the city walls to discourage the men inside.

But the victory had been only a skirmish. The sultan's main army was still on the way, and the walls had not even been dented. The main Turkish force arrived five days later.

Kilij Arslan had temporarily abandoned his quarrel with the Danisment emir. He directed an attack against the crusaders on May 21. Once again it was aimed at Raymond at the south gate. The battle raged all day. The Turks had the larger force, but in the flat plain they had no chance against the charge of the knights. By the end of the day the sultan was forced to withdraw. He sent a message to the defenders of the city. They would have to hold out as best they could alone.

With Kilij Arslan temporarily disposed of, the siege tightened. Robert of Normandy and Stephen of Blois joined the siege on June 3. They were sorely needed.

Despite the lack of reinforcements, the Turks fought courageously. Every day the Crusaders pressed against the walls, bringing up huge wooden towers, scaling ladders, and engines to hurl stones against the defenders. Every day they were thrown back with heavy losses, their towers destroyed by fire, hundreds of their men killed by Turkish archers.

At one point Raymond of Toulouse almost succeeded in breaking through the wall. His engineers began digging a tunnel under a weak tower, chipping away at the stone and then bringing up wood for a bonfire. The fire cracked the stone, and the tower toppled at sunset. But the Crusaders could not make an assault at night. By the next morning the Turks had repaired the damage.

It soon became clear that the siege was hopeless unless something could be done about the supplies coming into the city from the lake. The Crusaders went to Alexius to see if he could do anything about it. It was the moment Alexius had been waiting for. It proved to the Crusaders that they were helpless without him.

Alexius' solution to the problem was to drag boats overland from the coast and man them with Byzantine marines. The last Turkish escape route was finally cut off.

The defenders knew it was only a matter of time then. They signaled the Byzantine commander on the lake and offered to negotiate. And Alexius, who was a master at that art, agreed.

Alexius offered generous terms. The Turkish garrison would be left alive and ransomed. The sultan's wife and children would be released unharmed. There would be no looting of the city.

These were the best terms the Turks could hope for. The Crusaders, who knew nothing about the negotiations, had been going ahead with plans for a general assault on the city, and Alexius encouraged them, promising to aid them with an attack on the lake side. On the day of the assault, the Turks opened the gates to the Byzantines on the lake. The Turks were taken into boats and smuggled across to the opposite shore, and the Byzantines entered the city.

As the Crusaders approached the walls for the final attack, they suddenly saw the Byzantine standards being raised over the city.

The word flashed through the Crusader ranks: the Byzantines had taken the city by assault from the lake. Joyfully the Crusaders broke off the attack and returned to their camp.

The joy turned to grumbling when they learned they were not going to be allowed to sack the city. They had fought hard, and loot was their only pay. But Alexius stopped some of the grumbling when he distributed presents and money among all the men. Bohemond and the other leaders probably knew the Byzantines had taken the city by a trick, but they didn't complain about being used. Their oaths would have required them to turn the city over to Alexius in any case. The trick, whatever it was, had saved the lives of hundreds of their men. And it was still a long way to Jerusalem.

The Crusaders stayed another week at Nicaea, resting and planning their next move. They met with Alexius and renewed their oaths. Alexius agreed to take their sick and wounded, and promised to join the Crusade with his own army in a few weeks. In the meantime, he would send Byzantine guides and a general named Taticius to lead the Crusaders to Antioch. The road south from Nicaea led through treacherous mountain passes and across deserts that would suck the life out of any army passing through them in summer.

The Crusaders accepted the guides gratefully, although they suspected that Taticius' real job was to spy on them. They were also joined by Peter the Hermit, who was determined to finish his pilgrimage in spite of the loss of most of his following. He was still held in awe by the common people, who saw him as a visible reminder that God had blessed their journey.

The army set out from Nicaea on June 26. They were burdened by large numbers of women and other noncombatants, and as always the problem of supplies plagued them. After a day's march they reached a bridge spanning the river Sangarius (Sakarya). There they split into two groups to make the supply problem easier. Bohemond and Robert of Normandy set out first, accompanied by Peter. The others followed a day later.

The split was a foolish move, but the Crusaders felt there was little danger from the defeated Kilij Arslan. It would be a long time before he could repair his shattered forces and threaten them again. But, then, the Crusaders knew very little about Muslim politics.

After his defeat, Kilij Arslan rode east again into the domains of the Danisment emir. This time the two Muslim princes settled their differences and joined forces to dispose of the Crusader invasion once and for all. The army they assembled was enormous. One chronicler numbered it at 360,000 men, which is ridiculously exaggerated. But if the army was only a fifth that size, it was still a formidable force. After Nicaea the Crusaders had somewhere around 5,000 knights and another 30,000 infantry, along with thousands of noncombatants. When the Crusaders split into two groups, each alone was badly outnumbered by the Turks.

On the night of June 30, Bohemond and Robert made camp in a valley near Dorylaeum (Eskisehir). They had been watched all day by Turkish scouts who reported their moves to Kilij Arslan. The next morning the Crusaders set out at dawn. They had barely started when scouts sent ahead by Bohemond reported a host of Turks moving into position in the surrounding hills. Bohemond ordered the pack animals stripped and the camp set up again near a marsh which would protect their flank. He sent a message to Raymond and Godfrey. "Come quickly," he told them, "if you would fight alongside us this day."

The women and children were assembled in the center of the camp with the priests and a detachment of foot soldiers assigned to guard them. Bohemond, Robert, and Stephen of Blois rode out with their knights to meet the Turks. They were stunned by what they saw.

On the hills on every side, file after file of Turkish cavalry emerged. Unlike the Crusaders, they all had horses, and they were armed with short, powerful bows. Bohemond brought his men up on line and stood fast, anticipating the Turkish charge. Only one man disobeyed his orders. Robert of Paris spurred his horse forward and, followed by about forty of his knights, drove with his lance toward the Turks. They broke before him and then swallowed him up. Only a few of his men managed to cut their way back to the Crusader lines. Robert of Paris died in the charge.

Slowly, with his knights leading, Bohemond began to advance.

The Turks had learned their lesson at Nicaea. Rather than charge the Frankish knights, they sent their archers out in ranks, one behind the other. As each rank fired, the next one came up to take its place while the first retreated. Arrows fell in the Crusader ranks like rain. Hardest hit were the horses, who went down with their riders, plunging and screaming in pain. Above the tumult the Turks sent up their war cry—a harsh guttural chattering that struck terror into the Crusaders. It seemed to them that they were facing the very devils of hell.

Within minutes the Crusaders and their camp were surrounded. Again and again they charged the Turkish ranks, only to be smothered by the endless ranks of Turkish cavalry. With their horses shot from under them, the knights continued to fight on foot. And then, with their bows spent, the Turks closed. Their curved scimitars clashed against the long swords of the Franks. The slaughter on both sides was appalling.

One group of Turks broke through the ranks of the foot soldiers guarding the camp, and for a while the scene at Cibotus was played all over again. The Turks fell on the women and priests in the camp and began the massacre.

The knights fell back. Under the press, Bohemond ordered a retreat to a new defensive line near the tents. The Turks who had broken through scuttled back, thinking the retreat was an attack on them.

Smelling an easy victory, Kilij Arslan pushed forward with the last of his reserves. He had brought with him the ropes he intended to use for binding the captives he would take. His confidence was premature.

For the Franks held. As the sun climbed in the sky, they beat off one attack after another. At the end of six hours, they were exhausted, toppling from the heat as much as from the Turkish swords. The priests worked over the dead and dying, women struggled to bring water to the men on the line, and even young boys, squires of the knights they served, joined the battle. So they fought on.

And then, suddenly, the blare of trumpets sounded on the hills above the plain. The standards of Toulouse and Bouillon and those of Hugh of Vermandois appeared. Raymond and Godfrey and Hugh had finally arrived. They broke the line of the Turks and joined Bohemond and the crippled army. The men with Bohemond and Robert took new heart. With their remaining horses, they gathered themselves for one more charge.

The Turks re-formed, but almost instantly they had to turn to meet a new threat. Bishop Adhemar of Le Puy, who had stood with Urban that first day, had taken another division of knights and circled around to the Turks' rear. Now it was they who were surrounded.

What had looked like certain defeat for the Crusaders turned into a rout of the Turks. They broke ranks and ran. The Crusaders pursued them all the way to their camp, killing them by the hundreds. The Turks abandoned their camp intact, and scattered in every direction.

When the Crusaders broke into the Turkish camp, they found an immense treasure. More important than the silver and gold was the number of horses, cattle, sheep, and camels that had been tethered and left behind. The Crusaders gathered it all.

The victory had been won at a terrible cost. Among the dead was Tancred's brother, William, and hundreds of others who were not named.

For two days the crusaders stayed at Dorylaeum to rest and bury their dead. They had a new respect for their enemy now. An anonymous chronicler who accompanied Bohemond wrote, "Who is wise or learned enough to describe the valor, skill, and fortitude of the Turks?" But he added quickly, "If they had clung to the true faith of Christ, no people could be found to equal them in strength of war. But by God's grace we overcame them."

The moral was clear. The Crusaders were certain that God had given them the victory. Now, nothing could stop them. They had no idea that the worst was to come. Stephen of Blois wrote home to his wife Adele, "In five weeks we shall reach Jerusalem unless Antioch resists us."

6

the walls of antioch

Antioch (Antakya) lay at the southeast corner of Asia Minor, the gateway to Syria and Lebanon. In Roman times it had been the third-largest city in the world, after Alexandria and Rome itself. It had been the site of the first Christian bishopric, founded by Saint Peter. At the end of the eleventh century it was still a magnificent city. Its amphitheater and marble baths, its churches and forums were surrounded by a massive wall, thirty feet high and wide enough to allow two chariots to pass side by side. Next to Antioch, the battlements of Nicaea faded into tiny barricades by comparison.

But between the Crusaders and the walls of Antioch were five hundred miles of deserts, mountain ranges, and Turkish fortresses. The Byzantines had once ruled this country, but it had been twenty years since the Turks overran it. It was the middle of summer, and the road was uncertain. Taticius warned the leaders of the Crusade that a difficult and dangerous journey lay before them.

To make matters worse, Kilij Arslan retreated from Dorylaeum burning and ravaging the country along the Crusaders' route. The

49

wells were filled in or poisoned, cisterns were smashed, and anything that might be used for food was driven off or destroyed.

The Crusaders set out from Dorylaeum on July 3 in a single body. They moved slowly, sometimes making as little as eight miles in a day. By the end of the month, the blazing heat and famine had begun to take their toll. The first to die were the horses and pack animals. Soon there was fever as well as famine. Raymond of Toulouse was stricken and came so close to dying that he was given the last rites. The women who had proved themselves at Dorylaeum dropped along the roadside and did not rise up again. A trail of graves followed the Crusader route like guideposts.

In the midst of the suffering, the common people, who made up the bulk of the army, grew closer together. But rifts were beginning to appear among the leaders. Bohemond began to mutter against Taticius, who was a natural scapegoat. Raymond of Toulouse, on the other hand, stoutly defended the Byzantines. The real quarrel between them, of course, had nothing to do with Taticius. Both were ambitious. After Dorylaeum, Bohemond was emerging as the natural leader of the Crusade. Raymond was fiercely jealous. The one man who might have healed the quarrel, Godfrey of Bouillon, was in the hospital train, mauled by a bear during a hunting expedition. And the two Roberts could only watch with growing apprehension.

By September 10, the army had reached the last great barrier between them and Antioch, a tall range of mountains cut by treacherous passes, and made almost impassable by the winter rains that were just starting. Taticius advised a roundabout route, swinging north into country that was populated mostly by Armenian Christians. From there they could cut through the mountains by the pass known as the Syrian Gates. Most of the army accepted the advice, but Tancred and Godfrey's brother Baldwin had grown sick of the journey. They broke off from the army and marched south to conquer territories for themselves.

Baldwin and Tancred moved swiftly in separate groups, unhampered by women or baggage. Within days Tancred reached the coastal city of Tarsus. There he easily drove off the small Turkish garrison, and was welcomed as a liberator by the mostly

Christian population. But Tancred had barely had time to take the city when Baldwin rode up with his army. Baldwin ordered Tancred to turn the city over to him. Tancred was furious. The city was his by right of conquest, but Baldwin had more men. Tancred was forced to submit.

Tancred went on to conquer Adana and Mamistra (Misis), two cities to the east, but he never forgave Baldwin for the theft of his city. It was the first time personal ambition had almost led to blows between leaders of the Crusade. It would not be the last.

Baldwin soon abandoned Tarsus, leaving a small garrison behind, and rejoined the main army at Marash (Maras). There he found his wife and children dying of fever. He stayed just long enough to see them buried, and struck out again for the east. This time he did not return.

In the meantime, the main army had crossed the pass over the Anti Taurus mountains with heavy losses. The last of the horses and most of the baggage had been lost on the steep cliffs. Sickness, cold, and hunger had taken thousands of people. By the time the army emerged into the plain of Antioch, one man in seven who had set out from Dorylaeum was dead. The casualties among the women were even worse.

But at the sight of the great city with its hundreds of towers, and the discovery that the land around was rich with food, the Crusaders forgot their misery and pressed forward. On October 20, the bishop of Le Puy led a force across the Iron Bridge spanning the Orontes (Asi) River. The next day they stood before the city walls.

The city of Antioch was shaped like a rough oval. One long side faced northwest, fronting a plain and the river, which curved close to the city wall. The opposite side climbed steep hills, broken by deep gulleys, which had been filled and bridged by the wall. At the highest point, a tall citadel looked down over the roofs of the city. Five gates opened into the plain on the river side. A sixth led into the wilderness of hills to the southeast.

The Crusaders' military problem was complex. Their siege engines were not large enough to damage the walls; indeed those walls had stood unbroken for centuries. The size of the city made it impossible to surround. And there were still a number of

Turkish fortresses in the hills. So at the beginning, the army settled into camps before the three gates on the north side. The two Roberts were held in reserve behind Bohemond's camp.

The Turkish forces in the city were commanded by Yaghi-Siyan, who had ruled as governor for the past ten years. As he watched the Crusaders setting up their camp, he must have wondered why they did not make an immediate assault on the city; he was certainly not prepared for one. He did not have enough men to defend the entire wall. He had heard of the disaster at Dorylaeum, and he knew that reinforcements would be a long time coming. But as the days passed and the Crusaders made no move, he grew bolder. His spies had told him what was happening. There was trouble in the Crusader camp.

The trouble was Bohemond. From the first moment he saw Antioch, he had privately sworn to make it his own. The only thing standing in the way of his ambition was the oath he had given to Alexius. Unfortunately, the other barons took their oaths seriously. Bohemond would need their support, and the only way he could get it was to show that Alexius had betrayed them somehow. And he would have to come up with a plan to take the city himself.

Raymond of Toulouse was the only leader who urged an immediate attack. Bohemond argued eloquently that they were too weak after the march over the mountains. Besides, Alexius had promised to join them. It would be safer to wait. Bohemond won the argument, and the opportunity for a quick victory was lost.

The Crusaders spent the first three weeks of the siege gathering food from neighboring villages, and gorging themselves after the long famine. A lake was found nearby where the men could find relief from the still lingering heat. Some of the lords returned to their favorite peacetime occupation—hunting with falcons and dogs. As the days dragged by, and the Turks hid quietly behind their walls, the Crusaders settled into the routine of camp life. But the inactivity was paralyzing. Old quarrels flared up among the men. The foraging parties grew careless, wandering from the camp without guards. Prostitutes from the city and neighboring villages began visiting the tents.

While the Crusaders stagnated across the river, Yaghi-Siyan

was busily laying in supplies and strenghtening his fortifications. In the early part of November he sent small patrols out from the unguarded gates. The patrols waited in the hills and by the lake, and ambushed small groups and single Crusaders wandering alone. Soon he was sending larger patrols. Skirmishes broke out, and the elusive Turks usually had the best of them.

October slipped away, and then November. The weather changed. The heat softened and the skies turned gray. Rain fell in steady drizzles, turning the camp into a sea of mud. With the rains came sickness again. And still there was no word from Alexius.

By December the Crusaders were faced with a familiar problem. Food was growing short again. They had not laid in enough supplies, and most of the country around Antioch had been picked clean. The foraging parties had to venture even farther into Turkish territory, which was becoming increasingly dangerous. The men were restless, and a few of the weaker sort were beginning to desert.

Shortly before Christmas, the leaders met in council to decide what must be done. Stephen of Blois was elected head of the council, partly because he was well liked, and partly because he could stand between Bohemond and Raymond. Their quarrel had grown into open hatred. Godfrey was still sick, and Robert of Normandy was away on the coast, where some English ships were attacking the port of St. Symeon (Samandag).

Bohemond summed up the situation. They could not last the winter without supplies and reinforcements. There were rumors about a large Turkish relief force being gathered by the powerful regent of Mosul (Al Mawsil). The lords of Damascus and Aleppo (Halab) were also sending men to aid the Turks of Antioch.

Short of abandoning the Crusade, there was only one solution. They would have to divide forces, with Raymond and Godfrey's men staying with the siege, while Bohemond and Robert of Flanders took a large force south into Syria. They would raid towns and bring back all the food they could lay their hands on.

The plan was adopted, and Bohemond set out on December 28 with 15,000 men, half the remaining strength of the army. They had little luck at first, finding most of the Syrian villages deserted, and almost no food. Then on the last day of the year, as they were approaching a small village, they unexpectedly ran into the Turkish relief force coming up from Damascus.

The Crusaders were taken completely by surprise. Robert of Flanders, who was in the lead, was almost surrounded. He stood his ground, and the Turks pressed forward to divide the two halves of the army. Bohemond waited until the Turks were committed, and then charged. The Turkish attack was smashed, and once again the survivors scattered.

But the victory was hollow. Bohemond and Robert were forced to return to Antioch nearly empty-handed. They found the camp deep in gloom, and a number of fresh graves dotting the cemetery.

Yaghi-Siyan had taken advantage of Bohemond's absence and sent out a large force to attack the camp. Raymond had reacted just in time, driving the Turks back into the city. But a large number of knights had been killed. The next day an earthquake had struck, and signs were seen in the sky. The news of Bohemond's failure was the last blow to the Crusader morale. The desertions increased daily.

Tancred returned from his adventures in the north with news of Alexius and Baldwin. Alexius was making his way toward Antioch slowly, securing Turkish forts and towns the Crusaders had bypassed. Baldwin had struck deep into northern Syria, taking the city of Edessa (Urfa). The news was welcome, but it did not improve conditions in the camp, which were growing desperate.

A trickle of supplies came in from the port that Robert of Normandy and the English seamen had captured, but it was not nearly enough to feed the mass of men and women outside Antioch. Food was sold at fantastic prices. Some of the poorer knights were forced to butcher their captured horses. Some men boiled bark stripped from trees, and others chewed hopelessly at thorns. Hundreds died.

In January Peter the Hermit slipped out of his tent one night, and started down the road to Constantinople. Tancred noticed his absence and pursued. Peter was dragged back to the camp, but his attempted desertion was smoothed over. Things were bad enough without shaming Peter openly. Many of the common folk were already beginning to wonder if God had not deserted them as well.

Then one morning in February, it was discovered that Taticius had disappeared. Bohemond loudly proclaimed that this was just one more example of Byzantine treachery and cowardice. But Taticius' story was slightly different. He later claimed that Bohemond had come into his tent the night before and warned him that a murder plot was being hatched. The Crusaders were blaming the Byzantines for their troubles. It would be safer for Taticius if he was not around when their anger boiled over. Taticius took the hint.

February was the darkest month of the siege. A second Turkish relief force arrived from Aleppo and joined Yaghi-Siyan's forces for a two-pronged attack. Once again, Bohemond took charge. He ordered the foot soldiers to remain at the camp and hold off the Turks from the city. With 700 knights, all that was left in any condition to fight, Bohemond took up positions behind the Iron Bridge. The passage was narrow, with the lake on one side and the river on the other to protect the Crusaders' flanks. The Turkish force numbered about 7,000, but in the cramped space, they would have to attack in narrow ranks.

The first line of knights charged as the Turks came up on the bridge. The Crusaders were thrown back, and the Turks followed in hurried disorder—straight into the flat ground where Bohemond was waiting for them.

Godfrey was there, recovered from his illness, and the two Roberts and Tancred. Their swords sung, splitting through the light armor of the Turks. They fought like madmen, and within an hour it was over. Only the lack of horses prevented the Crusaders from capturing the Turkish camp intact.

In the meantime, the foot soldiers had held just as fiercely against the Turkish attack on the camp. When Yaghi-Siyan learned the fate of the relief force, he withdrew back into the city.

The battle was a turning point in the siege. As February ended, the rains ceased, and some of the sick men began to recover. A fleet of ships put in at the port, and they were loaded with materials for building siege engines and towers. By the middle of

March the Crusaders had constructed forts opposite the unguarded gates, and Yaghi-Siyan finally found himself bottled up inside his city.

The Turks had suffered terrible losses in the battles, and as their supplies were cut off, they began to suffer from hunger as well. From the middle of March, it was only a question of time.

But time was working against the Crusaders too. Spring brought relief from the famine, but it also brought news of Kerbogha and the great Muslim army of Mosul. Kerbogha had gathered 30,000 men. In their weakened condition, the Crusaders would not have a chance against such a host.

By May Kerbogha was at Edessa, where he was being held up temporarily by Baldwin. The Turks in Antioch showed no signs of cracking, although food in the city was almost gone. And what had been despair in the Crusader ranks was rapidly turning to panic. On June 2, Stephen of Blois, head of the council, optimist, who had written so cheerily to his wife even in the darkest times, bolted.

7

the holy lance

Bohemond prowled the edge of the camp, surveying the ragged tents and the clotted mud, and gnashed his teeth in frustration. He did not fear the Turks or death. The thing that nearly drove him mad was the sight of the great prize, so nearly in his grasp. All his life he had dreamed of ruling such a city. And now the dream was to be crushed.

It was the middle of May. Kerbogha was at Edessa, pounding at the walls as Baldwin showered stones and Greek fire on his men. He would not be held up there for long.

Time. That was the problem. If only they had more time. Bohemond returned to his tent, his face darkened with gloom. In his tent he was surprised to find a stranger—an Armenian dressed like a Turk. The sight was not really so strange. The camp was flooded with refugees and native Christians. The man said he wished to speak to Bohemond privately. He had a message from someone in the city.

Bohemond listened as the man spoke—in low tones. There were spies everywhere. Bohemond nodded, asked questions, and then the man slipped away. When Bohemond came out of his tent, he was smiling.

At a council of the barons the same day, Bohemond offered a proposition. "We are all suffering," he said, "from the worst sort of poverty and misery. Therefore let us elect one man to head the rest, and if he can manage to capture the city, let us bestow it on him as a gift."

The suggestion was stiffly rejected. Raymond of Toulouse was especially opposed to it. "We have all shared equally in the suffering; we will share equally in the prize."

Bohemond shrugged, and outside he laughed again. During the next days he met several times with the messenger from the city. Kerbogha abandoned his siege of Edessa, and advanced on Antioch. The news of his approach spread panic.

On the day Stephen of Blois packed up his tent and deserted the Crusade, Bohemond met with the council again. Kerbogha's advance guard had been sighted. His army would be at the Iron Bridge within two days at most. There was no time for argument. If Bohemond could figure out a way to capture the city, he could have it. The only dissenting vote was cast by Raymond.

With the majority of the barons behind him, Bohemond rapidly sketched out his plan. That afternoon, a large force of Crusaders marched off to the southwest, as if they were going to intercept Kerbogha. The Turks on the walls watched them go and relaxed.

When the sun went down, Bohemond ordered a halt. Away from the prying ears of spies in the camp, Bohemond told Robert of Flanders and Godfrey that he had been in contact with a man named Firouz, an officer in the city who commanded one of the towers. Firouz was a renegade who hated Yaghi-Siyan and was willing to betray him.

Under the cover of darkness, Bohemond and his followers slipped through the hills, back toward the wall and the place known as the Tower of the Two Sisters. They found a rope ladder dropped from the tower and a panicky Firouz, who urged them to hurry. A French knight named Fulk was the first up the ladder. He was followed by Robert of Flanders and about sixty others. Firouz was in an agony of fear. "You are too few," he hissed. "Where is Bohemond?"

A Norman knight came down the ladder and ran to where

Bohemond was standing. "It is time," the knight said. "We already hold three towers."

Bohemond scrambled up the rope. The rest crowded and pushed after him. Under their weight, the ladder broke. It hardly mattered. In the dark, they groped to the nearest gate, which was thrown open by the men inside. The Crusaders charged into the city. Within minutes they had captured the main gates. Raymond and the rest of the army were waiting. Trumpets sounded. "God wills it!"

Antioch was theirs.

Yaghi-Siyan woke to the sounds of fighting and knew that the battle was lost. He grabbed a horse and fled into the hills. His horse threw him, and he was found, still stunned from his fall, by some Armenian peasants. They recognized him and killed him where he lay.

The Crusaders scattered through the city, grabbing loot and killing every Turk they found. The Armenians and other Christians rose up to help them. The only part of the city which put up any resistance was the citadel. Bohemond personally led the attack on the stone tower. It failed miserably. Bohemond was carried down the hill, bleeding from a wound in the hip.

As the sun rose that morning, the third of June, the Crusaders went mad with joy. They had captured the city intact. The fortifications stood between them and Kerbogha. And never had they seen such wealth. All day they surged through the palaces and mosques, gathering gold and silver plate, fine cloth and treasures from the East—for Antioch had been a great trading city. But night fell, and Bohemond knew they were little better off than they had been outside the walls. There were no stores of food left in the city. In a few hours the port would be closed. Since the citadel had not been taken, they would have to face the Turks from both front and rear.

Bohemond bound up his wound and began making preparations for the coming battle. A barricade was thrown across the steep path leading down from the citadel. A group of knights under Roger of Barneville volunteered to go to the Iron Bridge and hold up the Turks as long as they could. And Robert of Flanders went out from the city to defend the tower they had built during the siege.

A few horses had been captured from the Turks, and these were assigned to Tancred, who commanded the only mounted knights.

The preparations were barely completed when the first Turks came to the Iron Bridge. Roger of Barneville's suicidal defense ended in death for himself and all his men. By June 7, Kerbogha and the main Muslim army were at the walls.

Kerbogha did not waste any time. Men were sent to reinforce the Turks still holding the citadel, and on June 9 they launched a furious assault against the Crusaders' rear. Hugh of Vermandois and Robert of Normandy defended the makeshift barricade. The attack nearly broke through, but again the narrow passage hindered the Turks. Nightfall ended the battle, with the Crusaders still holding the barricade.

Robert of Flanders had also managed to hold out for a day in the tower opposite the Bridge Gate. On the second day the Turks brought up siege engines. Robert set fire to the tower and retreated with most of his men under the covering smoke. They were safe behind the walls, but Kerbogha had completed his encirclement of the city.

The leaders of the Crusade met in council again. They knew their situation was desperate. There was no food. The morale of the men was lower than it had been during the darkest days in February. And there was still no sign of Alexius.

Once again Bohemond took charge. At a public gathering he loudly vowed that he would never surrender Antioch—not if he was locked up inside for seven years. The other leaders took the same oath. Tancred added that as long as he had forty knights to follow him, he would not turn back until they had taken Jerusalem.

The oaths steadied the nerves of some of the wavering men. Words could not stop Kerbogha, though. He pressed the attack daily, probing the wall for weak points. The Crusaders were forced to defend their positions constantly. They were soon worn out by the attacks and the hunger that gnawed at all of them. On the fifth day of the siege, the desertions began again.

Singly and in groups men slipped over the walls at night and attempted to work through the Turkish lines. Most were caught and brutally tortured, but a few got away. They fled north—toward Constantinople and Alexius, who was finally coming to the rescue with the Byzantine army.

Alexius had met Stephen of Blois on the road. Stephen reported the scene at Antioch in the blackest terms. He had stuck around just long enough to know that the Crusaders had taken the city. He had also seen—from a safe distance—Kerbogha's army approaching.

"Surely all our men are dead," Stephen said. He urged the emperor to turn back.

Alexius listened to Stephen's story and considered. So far the Crusade had done very well for him. He had recaptured vast territories from the Turks. To throw away his army now, in a useless rescue attempt when the men were already dead, would be insane. The deserters from Antioch confirmed Stephen's story. Alexius ordered his men to pack up and return to Constantinople.

Behind the walls of Antioch, Bohemond knew nothing of this. He directed the defense with furious energy. At night he walked the streets and rousted out malingerers. On one occasion he found some men sleeping in a house after the alarm signaling an attack had sounded. He ordered the men out, but they refused. They were starving, exhausted, and ready to die. Bohemond set fire to the house. When the men stumbled out, choking and blinded by the smoke, Bohemond drove them toward the walls with the flat of his sword.

But Bohemond could not solve the real problem with his sword. The Crusaders had set out on a war they believed had been approved by God. As long as He was with them, they had come through over terrible odds. Now it was clear that God had abandoned them. It had happened to Emich and to Peter's men at Cibotus because of their sins. It was happening again here at Antioch. It was a time when belief held more power than swords or lances. None of the leaders' determination or Bohemond's ferocity would change that.

It would take a miracle.

Because they believed in miracles, and because they hoped so desperately for one, a miracle came to them—of a sort. Feverish with hunger and exhaustion, some of the men began to experience visions. One man reported that he was attempting to desert when he was stopped by the ghost of his dead brother. The ghost had told him to turn back because the Turks would be defeated and the city would be saved in a few days. Other visions were widely reported. Then one day a poor pilgrim named Peter Bartholomew came to Bishop Adhemar of Le Puy and Raymond to tell them of a vision he had seen of Saint Andrew.

The saint had told Peter that Christ had heard the Crusaders' prayers and was ready to aid them. And so the people would know that this was true, a sign would be given to them. Buried deep in the ground under a certain church in Antioch was a lance—the same lance, in fact, that had been used by the Roman soldier who had pierced Christ's side at the crucifixion. If the Crusaders dug under the church, they would find the lance. They must make an attack on the Turks, carrying the lance before them like a banner, and Christ would scatter their enemies.

The bishop of Le Puy heard Peter's story, and flatly denounced him as a liar. Peter was an unsavory sort, reputed to be a drunkard and hardly the type Saint Andrew would choose to visit. But Peter insisted he was telling the truth. Raymond was impressed with the story and thought it was worth investigating. A dozen men went to the church Peter had identified and began to dig. The excavation went on all day without turning up anything. Peter insisted they continue, and finally he jumped into the hole himself to help. Moments later he made his discovery. It was a rusted piece of iron—a broken spear point with the shaft missing, but clearly identifiable as a lance.

News of the discovery flashed through the city. Bishop Adhemar was still skeptical, but he held his tongue. This was the miracle they had been waiting for. Instantly the Crusaders' morale underwent a complete change. That morning they had been broken, despairing, and ready to give up. That evening they were thronging the churches, singing with joy, and ready to overwhelm the Turks. Their leaders could barely restrain them.

Bohemond may not have believed in the lance—the fact that Peter had been the man to come up with it when the others could find nothing was suspicious—but he recognized its value. He decided the time had come to strike.

A five-day fast was ordered by the priests as a sign of repentance. During those five days, preparations were made for the final attack.

On June 27, Peter the Hermit was sent to the Turkish camp. No one knows what he had to say to Kerbogha, but it is known that he returned with a message from the Turkish leader. Kerbogha promised that any of the Crusaders who accepted Islam would be well treated. The rest would become slaves for the Muslim princes of the East.

Bohemond laughed at the terms. Not one man from the city went out to surrender. On the next day, June 28, the priests put on their white robes, spoke the words of the Mass for the last time, and began to lead a procession toward the Bridge Gate.

Bohemond had drawn up the army in six groups. Hugh of Vermandois and Robert of Flanders led the first group. Following them were Godfrey, Robert of Normandy, Bishop Adhemar, Bohemond, and Tancred. Raymond stayed in the city to guard their rear against the Turks in the citadel.

The men marched silently, their banners fluttering in the wind. At their head, at the very front of the line, a priest carried the lance, also like a banner. It was the banner they all looked to.

While the Crusaders were filing out of the city, Kerbogha was playing chess in his tent. One of his officers broke in and warned that the Crusaders were coming. Kerbogha asked if they intended to fight. The officer invited him to see for himself.

Kerbogha watched as the first line of Crusaders came out, followed by the second and third. "Shouldn't we attack them at once before they have time to form?" the officer asked.

"Let them all come out, and we will be done with them at one stroke."

Adhemar emerged with the lance, then Bohemond and Tancred with the cavalry.

"We may kill them," Kerbogha's officer remarked. "But they will never be put to flight."

The lines spread out left and right to form a single rank, with Adhemar and the lance at the center. The Turks fired their arrows, and men fell. But the ranks did not waver. They marched steadily toward the Turks. They cared for nothing—certainly not death. On the left, a squadron of Turkish cavalry attempted to circle around the Crusader flank. They were thrown back by Godfrey and Robert of Normandy.

And from the mountains, the Crusaders imagined they saw another rank of horsemen. Their horses and their armor were white. The pennants streaming from their lances were also white. They rode into the Turkish ranks, scattering and throwing them into confusion.

Fire broke out along the line—the signal for a Turkish retreat. The Crusaders ran forward, following the lance and screaming their battle cry. Tancred, with the only cavalry, spurred his horse. They charged.

The power of the Turks in northern Syria was broken that day. It would not rise up to challenge the Crusaders for another four decades. Kerbogha escaped to Mosul, and later died in disgrace—defeated by a rusty piece of iron.

Such was the power of belief.

8

the fall of jerusalem

Nothing was settled. The Turks had flown like a wisp of smoke, leaving their camp intact and the Crusaders masters over northern Syria. But the question remained, which of them was to rule it?

Bohemond had the clearest claim. The other barons had promised to support him if he took the city, and he had done it. But Raymond of Toulouse stubbornly held that the city belonged to Alexius. Raymond also held the Bridge Gate and the city palace with his army. Bohemond held the citadel, which had surrendered without a fight after Kerbogha's defeat. So unless Bohemond was willing to resort to open warfare, there was a stalemate.

The council could not reach a compromise. They were stuck in Antioch in any case. No one was willing to resume the journey to Jerusalem with the army weakened and the summer sun turning the country to the south into a virtual desert. So the Crusade stalled again, and nearly broke up.

One man had had enough. Hugh of Vermandois packed up a few days after the Battle of the Lance and set out for home. He carried letters and a message for Alexius. At the time, the Crusaders did not realize that Alexius had deserted them. It was hoped by some that the emperor would come and claim his city.

As it turned out, Hugh had to fight his way to Constantinople and did not meet Alexius until fall. Alexius must have been surprised and pleased to see his friend alive and to hear the news of Antioch. But there was no way he could come until spring. By then it would be too late.

In Antioch, an epidemic broke out in July. One of its first victims was Adhemar, the bishop of Le Puy. He died on August 1, and was buried sadly in the church where Peter Bartholomew had found the lance. He had been one of the most respected of the leaders. All the factions of the army had looked up to him, not only because of his heroic action at Dorylaeum, but because he was the symbol of the Church.

After Adhemar's death, the leaders scattered. Godfrey rode north to visit his brother Baldwin. Bohemond took a force to capture some of the towns around Antioch, most of which surrendered hastily at his approach. Robert of Normandy went south a little ways to the port of Latakia (Al Ladhiqiyah), where he presumably pursued his two favorite hobbies.

It was the middle of September when they met again. A letter was drawn up to be sent to Urban from all the leaders of the Crusade. They reported Adhemar's death and urgently requested the pope to come himself or send a replacement. Months later, the pope would appoint an Italian archbishop, Daimbert of Pisa, to take Adhemar's place. It was a choice the Crusaders would have cause to regret.

But for now the question of Jerusalem and Antioch remained. The army was growing restless. The common people began muttering among themselves. They had suffered more than anyone. Thousands of their friends were dead. They had not come for riches or to rule kingdoms. They had been moved by a vision of Jerusalem, and now they were being denied fulfillment because of their leaders' ambition. In January, they finally took matters into their own hands.

During December, Raymond and Bohemond had joined forces to take the city of Maarrat an Numan, several miles to the southeast of Antioch. As soon as the battle was over, they began quarreling again. Raymond's troops had done most of the fighting, but the city was in the territory of Antioch. Both men claimed it.

Each left part of his army to guard the city and returned to Antioch to continue the argument. Winter was bringing another famine; the men were ready to revolt. The soldiers and pilgrims met at Maarrat and discussed what to do.

"Quarrels over Antioch," they muttered. "Quarrels over Maarrat. Is this to happen in every city God gives us? Let us end it now by destroying this city."

Over the protests of the knights, the common people began tearing down the walls. Raymond heard of the destruction and hurried back. He saw the ruined wall, he heard the complaints, and he was finally moved to shame. On January 13, 1099, Raymond ordered fire to be set to the city to complete the destruction. He dressed himself in pilgrim's robes and walked barefoot at the head of the people. He finally turned his face toward Jerusalem.

Raymond had 300 knights and perhaps 2,000 foot soldiers under his command. The mass of pilgrims who had survived, about 5,000 in all, were behind him. Tancred hurried up with his forty knights to fulfill his vow, and a few days later, Robert of Normandy followed. Bohemond stayed at Antioch, which belonged unquestionably to him now. A month later, Godfrey and Robert of Flanders also hurried toward Jerusalem.

Raymond's change of heart had been sudden, and there was something theatrical about his gesture. But it had been the common people who had provided the spark for the Crusade. Perhaps something of their spirit had passed into Raymond. If so, it was appropriate that he should go as a pilgrim. At the head of the procession, Raymond carried the lance of Antioch. And behind it marched those other two symbols, Peter Batholomew and Peter the Hermit. This time they would not be deflected from their course.

They were a pathetic parade, but the Arabs and Turks in the cities they passed trembled at their approach. No one knows how many of them had set out from Europe; it may have been as many as 200,000. Most were dead, a few scattered in garrisons around Antioch and Edessa. The remnant, with their bony horses and ragged banners, hardly looked like an army. The surviving pilgrims, several thousand women and unarmed men, straggled behind them. Yet this ragged army had mauled the finest forces of Islam. Already the legends were growing among the Muslims. Kerbogha's officer had expressed the feeling: they could be killed, but they could not be defeated. Few along their route cared to try.

Envoys were sent from the towns with tribute and offers of alliance. In some cases the towns were simply abandoned. In February, they came to the rich coastal city of Tripoli (Tarabulus), and there the changeable Raymond caused them to stall again.

Raymond had decided that Tripoli was too rich a prize to pass up. Before they could take the city, though, they would have to secure the fortress of Arqa, which guarded the northern approach to Tripoli. The army sat outside Arqa for two months without making any progress. They had lost all heart for these side adventures. The attack was not pressed very hard.

It was at Arqa that Raymond was joined by Godfrey and Robert of Flanders. They were now as anxious to push on to Jerusalem as the pilgrims. They urged Raymond to abandon the siege. Robert of Normandy and Tancred agreed with them, but Raymond was stubborn. It looked like the old quarrels from Antioch might flare up again.

Then, as at Antioch, Peter Bartholomew came forward to change the course of events. After the Battle of the Lance, Peter had emerged as a hero of the common people. Raymond of Toulouse had practically adopted Peter, keeping him by his side at all times. Raymond even allowed Peter to sleep in his tent so Peter could report his dreams instantly. For the visions had not ended after Antioch. More and more they were becoming commands from heaven which tended to support Raymond of Toulouse. At one point Peter claimed to have seen the dead bishop, Adhemar, who showed Peter his burned hands and face—a punishment from hell, since Adhemar had not believed in the lance. And now Peter came to the barons outside Arqa and told them he had been visited by Saint Andrew again. This time the saint ordered them to make an immediate assault on Arqa.

The Normans were getting a little sick of Peter and his visions. They laughed and called him a liar. They suggested the lance was probably a fraud as well. Peter was furious. Apparently he genuinely believed in his visions. He challenged the army to test him. He said he would undergo the ordeal by fire.

The army agreed to the test. On Good Friday, two huge fires were built with a narrow path separating them. The fires were so hot the surrounding crowd could not approach closer than a few feet. Peter had to run directly through the path between the two fires. If he came out unburned, it would be proof that God was protecting him and he had not lied.

Stripped to the waist and carrying the holy lance in one hand, Peter dashed through the fire. He made it to the other side, but he was badly burned and he fell. Some of the witnesses blamed his injuries on the crowd, who pressed up against him when he emerged from the fire. Others simply said he had failed the test. No one will ever know the truth. Twelve days after his ordeal, Peter died, and the lance was generally forgotten. Only Raymond continued to believe in it. He carried it with him in a silver case, and eventually presented it to Alexius. From there it disappeared forever.

In May, Raymond was forced to give in to the pressure and abandon the siege of Arqa. The army passed Tripoli, and three days later they came to Beirut. There they entered for the first time country ruled by the Fatimid Arabs of Egypt.

The Fatimids were deadly enemies of the Turks, and they were anxious to make an alliance with the crusaders. The previous summer, they had taken advantage of the Turkish troubles in the north to capture Jerusalem from the Turkish garrison. The Arabs offered safe passage for any Crusaders who wished to visit Jerusalem. The offer was rejected. The Crusaders were not interested in visits. They meant to rule.

The Crusaders passed Sidon (Sayda) and Tyre (Sure) with their lovely ports and strong citadels. Acre (Akko) sent them tribute, and at Ramla the inhabitants fled. From Ramla the Crusaders turned east. Tancred broke off from the main army with a hundred knights and raced toward Bethlehem. The Christians of the town came out to meet them singing with joy. By June 7, the joy had spread to the main army. They had reached Jerusalem.

It was not the city of their visions, or even the city they had heard described in the Bible, in a land "flowing with milk and honey." What they saw was a city much smaller than Antioch. It sat on a hill, flanked by deep gulleys and protected by an ancient wall. The countryside was dry and barren. The few wells had been filled in or poisoned by the Arabs. Streams had dried up under the blistering sun, and stinging flies added to the Crusaders' torment.

The lack of water was the greatest problem. The barons knew that a long siege would finish them. To add to their problems, the Muslims ejected the Christians of the city. They swelled the Crusader camp, but they were only extra mouths, useless for fighting. The refugees did bring news of conditions inside the city, and the news was not good. The Muslims were well supplied with food and water, and they had sent to Cairo for help.

The Crusaders launched their first attack on June 12. They broke through the low outer wall, but the main wall stopped them. They had only a few scaling ladders, and dozens of knights died hammering uselessly at the thick stone. The survivors withdrew.

A few days later, sailors from a Genoese fleet put in at the abandoned port of Jaffa (Tel Aviv). The ships brought supplies of food, but no materials for building siege engines. The desert heat and the lack of water was sucking the life out of the army. In the council, Tancred and Robert of Flanders volunteered to lead an expedition to the forests of the north and bring back wood for towers and ladders. Others scoured the countryside, and returned with precious supplies of water in goatskin bags.

The Crusaders worked with a kind of grim desperation. Hundreds who had survived famine at Antioch died of thirst at Jerusalem. As if to torment them, the Arabs had left one well open under the walls of the city, but it was within easy bowshot.

The siege lasted five agonizing weeks. Tancred and Robert brought back enough wood to construct dozens of mangonels, or catapults, and two towers, along with hundreds of scaling ladders. Then the siege began in earnest. The whir of stones flying through the air from the mangonels and the sounds of hammering echoed through the camp. The towers were set on wheels so they could be pushed against the walls. The front of the towers were covered with hides to protect the men inside. At the top, a swinging bridge was held up by ropes, ready to be dropped against the city wall when the ropes were cut.

By July 10, the towers were finished. They could not be wheeled into place, however, until a ditch near the south wall had been filled. For a night and a day the army labored to fill the ditch with stones, wood, dirt—anything they could find. The Arabs on the walls rained arrows and stones on them as they worked. The old men and the women flocked to help. When they dropped, others came forward to take their place.

On the fourteenth, the preparations were complete. The tower on the south was wheeled into place, commanded by Raymond. Godfrey of Bouillon and his brother Eustace stood atop the tower that would attack the north wall. Tancred and Robert of Normandy stood ready with scaling ladders before the Gate of St. Stephen. The attack began.

The Arabs fought fiercely, with fire, arrow, and stone. The men pushing the towers forward suffered the most. Both towers were short of the wall when night ended the battle. The Crusaders were forced to keep a strong guard around the towers through the night, lest the Arabs slip out of the city and set fire to them. But the Arabs spent the night building up the wall with timbers and setting up mangonels of their own. At dawn, the Crusaders resumed the assault.

The Arab machines took a terrible toll, and the Crusaders launched bundles of fire arrows, bound with iron rings, against them. Fires broke out all along the wall. The men pushing the towers strained, but on the south Raymond was stopped. Godfrey, Eustace, and a handful of knights stood on the second tower, screaming encouragement to the men below. They were only a few yards away. The tower cracked and lurched, and ground to a halt.

The fire along the wall had spread to the timbers thrown up

during the night. Flame and smoke obscured the wall, and in desperation Godfrey slashed at the ropes. The heavy wooden drawbridge dropped, caught against a projecting timber—and held.

Flame spread quickly to the tower. A knight named Lothold leaped through the flames, sword in hand. Godfrey and Eustace were right behind. They drove the Arabs before them.

Other Arabs came up to push them back, and the holes they left in the defenses allowed the men on the ladders to gain a foothold. The Crusaders swarmed over the walls. Robert of Normandy and a battering ram brought down the Gate of St. Stephen.

The battle was lost, but the Arabs put up a desperate fight, retreating through the streets to the temple of Solomon. Raymond of Toulouse finally broke through the south wall, where the Egyptian commander was personally directing the defense. The commander surrendered to Raymond with the usual conditions—that their lives would be spared. Raymond gave his promise.

By late afternoon the battle was over, and the massacre began. The Crusaders surged through the city, killing everyone they saw. Men, women, and children fell to their swords. The massacre continued through the night, with blood-spattered knights searching through every street and house for more victims. Only the men who had surrendered to Raymond survived.

Tancred captured one group of Muslims huddled together on the roof of a mosque. The terrified men surrendered to him, but refused to accompany him down to the streets, where the massacre was taking place. Tancred understood their fear. He left his banner with them as a sign of his protection. As soon as Tancred had left, another group of knights fell on the prisoners and slaughtered them all.

The Jews of the city were rounded up and herded into their synagogue. When the doors were shut behind them, fire was set to the building. Not one of their number survived.

The Arabs making a hopeless last stand at the temple were not allowed to surrender. A witness described the scene: "Our men rode in blood up to their knees."

By morning of the second day it was over. The Crusaders were spent, and there was no one left to kill.

Many excuses have been offered for this senseless slaughter. The army was half mad with thirst, exhaustion, and the fever that comes with battle. Yet the fact remains that they had taken other cities and fought other battles under conditions as bad without murdering women and children. The slaughter went on long after the fever was spent.

The leaders took no part in the massacre, but they did nothing to stop it, either. While their men were rampaging through the streets, Godfrey, the two Roberts, and Raymond went solemnly up to the Church of the Holy Sepulcher to offer thanks. The sounds of singing and the chants of the priests mingled with the screams of dying men and women. No one seems to have considered it an odd mixture. The Great Crusade had ended in blood and tragedy, but it would be many years before the Crusaders would express regret for their action.

9

defender
of the holy sepulcher

A song was heard in Baghdad—a song of grief and lamentation. Al-Quds, the Holy—the name given to Jerusalem by the Muslims—had fallen. The minstrels wept at the sufferings of the city and demanded revenge. The caliph and his court heard the song, and they too wept. But weeks passed, the tears dried, and no army set out to avenge the massacre. Al-Quds was a long way from Baghdad.

Despite the songs and tears, the loss of Jerusalem was not a disaster for the Muslim world. Jerusalem ranked only third, behind Mecca and Medina, in religious importance. Politically and economically, it had almost no value, except to serve as a buffer between Cairo and Baghdad.

The caliphs of those two cities had been divided by religious questions for years. Cairo was the home of the Shiites, or Fatimids, the Muslim sect that accepted no authority but the Koran. It was a splinter group, much smaller than the orthodox Sunnites, who accepted as equally valid the oral traditions that had grown up after Muhammad's death. The Fatimids clung fiercely to their religious beliefs and were the sworn enemies of the Sunnites of Baghdad and Damascus. Since the Fatimids had a strong army and a fleet to back them up, their independence went unchallenged.

Baghdad accepted the loss of Jerusalem stoically. The Muslims were, above all, fatalists. What Allah had willed must come to pass. If Allah had willed the loss of a city ruled by Fatimids, so be it. The Jews, Greeks, Romans, Byzantines, and Turks had all lost it in turn. When the time was right, the turn would come for these blue-eyed invaders from the West. Meanwhile they were just one more pawn on the political chessboard.

The Crusaders, of course, knew nothing of this. They saw the Muslims as a single bloc of heathens, and damned them all equally to hell. Egyptian, Arab, and Turk were lumped together under the single name Saracen—an old Latin word that meant the peoples of Syria. Soon they would learn of the Muslim divisions and turn them to their own advantage. For the moment they were concerned only with holding on to their conquest. They were not aware of their lowly place in the Muslim strategy. A week after they took the city, the barons met in council for the last time—to elect a king.

It may seem like an obvious move, but it was actually not an easy decision. The expedition to Jerusalem had been launched by the Church. It was no ordinary city, to be ruled by a feudal baron. The man who ruled should be someone who reported directly to the Holy Father in Rome—a patriarch. Or so argued the churchmen in the council. They had a strong case. If they had had an equally strong candidate—if Adhemar had been alive—they might have carried the point. But the barons, as much as they honored the Church, felt the military situation was much too precarious to give up the city to the clergy. They held the city and a small corridor to the sea. All around them, and separating them from the conquered lands in the north, were towns and fortresses still held by the Muslims. The ruler they elected must wield a sword.

The choice was narrowed quickly. Both Robert of Normandy and Robert of Flanders were ready to go home. That left Godfrey and Raymond as the only possible candidates.

Raymond was clearly unacceptable, even though he made no secret that the title "king of Jerusalem" was one he wanted and felt himself worthy of. But Raymond had caused too much trouble. His quarrels with Bohemond had almost broken up the Crusade. He had stalled outside Tripoli. Worst of all, he was still a friend of the betrayer, Alexius. So the electors settled on Godfrey.

At first Godfrey modestly refused the office. He could not, he said, "wear a golden crown in the place where Christ had worn a crown of thorns." After a day of resistance, which was probably more symbolic than real, Godfrey gave in. He would not accept the title of king. Instead, he chose to be called "Defender of the Holy Sepulcher." He was king in all but name.

But a king must have subjects, and Godfrey's were rapidly dwindling away. The two Roberts were packing, getting ready to return to Europe with all their armies. Raymond of Toulouse, who naturally took his defeat as an insult, was ready to leave too. Only Tancred remained at Godfrey's side.

Before they set out, however, word came from the south of a great Muslim army coming up from Egypt. They were camped at Ascalon (Ashkelon), a scant forty miles from Jerusalem. Godfrey pleaded with the barons to put off their departure until they had turned back the Egyptians. The two Roberts readily agreed, and Raymond, as soon as he learned the danger was serious, hurried down from his camp on the Jordan, where he was nursing his pride and dreaming of a kingdom.

On August 12, the Crusaders, who numbered 1,200 knights and 9,000 foot soldiers, neared Ascalon. In the morning they surprised some Arabs who were herding a large number of sheep, goats, and cattle toward the Muslim camp. They rounded up the animals and learned from the captive herdsmen that the Egyptians were in their tents, not expecting a battle. The Crusaders hurried forward.

The captured animals followed, raising a cloud of dust that could be seen for miles. The Crusaders tried to drive off the animals without luck. The Egyptians saw the dust cloud and were roused from their camp. They rode out, but they did not attack. Through the dust they saw thousands of riders, or what looked like riders, moving in a thick line toward them. They had mistaken the cattle for horsemen, and paused. The pause gave the Crusaders time to draw close and swing around on line.

The line stopped, and the dust settled. In the Egyptian ranks, the Crusaders could see green banners and the standard of the vizier, topped by a silver ball that looked like an apple. For a moment there was silence except for the snorting and pawing of horses.

Then a roar went up, and Robert of Normandy spurred his horse. Lance down, he charged alone—straight at the silver standard. He was swallowed up, and the startled knights had no choice but to follow. Seconds later they saw the vizier's standard go down. Robert had cut his way through and killed the standard-bearer.

With that single act, panic spread through the Egyptian ranks. The battle became a pursuit, and the threat to Jerusalem was turned back. With the Egyptians routed, the Crusaders turned toward the fortress of Ascalon. They could have taken it easily, but once again a quarrel broke out. Raymond claimed the fortress for himself, and Godfrey rightly argued that it belonged to the kingdom of Jerusalem. The two Roberts refused to intervene, and the opportunity was lost. The army returned to Jerusalem with Ascalon still in Egyptian hands. It would remain there, a thorn in the side of the kingdom, for another fifty-three years.

The day had come for departures. Godfrey watched sadly as Eustace and the two Roberts mounted their horses. He gave them each his hand willingly. They had endured much together.

Only Raymond's departure had not grieved Godfrey. Raymond had left a few days before to visit his friend Alexius. Along the way he passed Tripoli, and the sight of the city stirred the old dream.

The two Roberts carried messages for Urban, but they were messages he would never hear. The pope would die two weeks after the capture of Jerusalem—never knowing that the Crusade he had launched had succeeded. For the two Roberts there would be a hero's welcome, and Europe would stir once again to send badly needed reinforcements.

Eustace would return to his own lands and die rich and secure many years later. Robert of Flanders would find peace at home, but he would die within eleven years, still young, while crossing a swollen river. For Robert of Normandy there would never be peace. He would spend his last years fighting a losing battle with his brothers over Normandy, and die in prison—an old man, broken and almost forgotten.

In the months that followed, Godfrey spent most of his time in the saddle, fighting skirmishes with raiding Bedouin tribes, directing sieges, and holding court for the envoys from Muslim towns. Tancred gathered in the towns of Nazareth and Tiberias near the Sea of Galilee, which he held as the vassal of Godfrey.

The battle of Ascalon had convinced most of the natives that the Crusaders were invincible. They were perfectly willing to accept Godfrey as their new master, and he in turn guaranteed them their lands and their lives. Treaties were made with the coastal cities of Acre and Tyre. The fanaticism that had led to the massacre at Jerusalem was turned to diplomacy. Godfrey was learning the great lesson of the East. It was the only way his tiny upstart kingdom could survive.

Godfrey's greatest problems came from inside his own capital, where members of the Church were still squabbling over their rightful place. The Greek Orthodox Church had survived four hundred years of Muslim occupation, and its followers naturally saw themselves as the spiritual heirs of the city. But a Latin bishop, Arnulf of Marturano, had been appointed patriarch. Arnulf had a shady reputation, and the Greeks soon found good reason to fear him. One of his first acts was to confiscate all property belonging to the Greek Church and turn it to his own use. He even resorted to torture when the Greeks refused to give up the piece of the True Cross they had hidden. The True Cross was the most important relic in Christendom. It was above all a symbol to the common people—a visible symbol of the presence of Christ. It gave both prestige and strength to the men who held it. The Greeks complained to Godfrey, but he did nothing to curb Arnulf. The divisions between the Christians were turning into an impassable gulf.

Then, in December, unexpected visitors arrived in Jerusalem. Bohemond and Baldwin, Godfrey's brother, had come to fulfill their vows. With them was the Italian archbishop appointed by the pope to replace Adhemar. His name was Daimbert of Pisa.

Daimbert arrived in Jerusalem burning with a single idea. The churchmen who had argued against Godfrey were not the only ones who dreamed of a kingdom ruled by the Church. Daimbert was armed with special powers from the pope and a fleet of ships from his own city of Pisa. The men of those ships were utterly devoted to the papal legate. Daimbert had also taken time to make friends with Bohemond and Baldwin during the voyage from Antioch. He knew there was a growing rift between Bohemond and Godfrey, and he was already planning to turn that rift to his own use.

As soon as he arrived, Daimbert declared Arnulf's appointment as patriarch illegal and took over the position himself. The change did not improve matters for the Greeks and only made them worse for Godfrey. In Arnulf, Godfrey had at least had a strong supporter. Now Daimbert began a systematic campaign to have Godfrey deposed.

To demonstrate his power, Daimbert arranged with Bohemond and Baldwin to have them crowned rulers of Antioch and Edessa in a special ceremony. Bohemond's motives for the action were simple enough. He needed legal sanction to rule a city that was still claimed by the Byzantine emperor. The move put Godfrey in a peculiar position. If he submitted to a similar ceremony, it would make him, legally, the vassal of the Church. If he did not, he would be the only Latin prince in the East who ruled without the sanction of the Church. In the end, Godfrey was forced to submit. He could stand up to Muslim swords, but the intrigues of the churchmen defeated him. Daimbert even extracted a promise from Godfrey that he would leave the city and turn it over to the Church as soon as he had conquered another city of equal value.

Bohemond and Baldwin returned north after a few days, and Godfrey returned to the never-ending job of subduing the countryside.

A new century dawned, and Godfrey was laying plans for taking the great coastal cities still in Muslim hands. Fleets from Venice arrived, anxious to open up new trading ports. Godfrey welcomed them and promised large concessions in the towns they captured. Through the spring, preparations were made for an attack on Acre. In June, Godfrey gathered his small forces at

Ramla and was joined by Tancred. They would cut off the land approaches to Acre while the Venetians attacked from the sea.

It was not to be. At Ramla, Godfrey fell sick with fever. He was taken first to Jaffa, but his condition worsened. He was strapped to a litter and carried back to Jerusalem. For three weeks the fever burned in his body. He died on July 18, after a reign of only a year.

Godfrey had accomplished much, considering the pitifully small forces available to him. He had held together his kingdom and set the pattern of accommodation and gradual conquest which his successors would follow. He had lived up to his title.

A story is told by the historian William of Tyre which typifies Godfrey's reign. It is said that some Arab sheikhs once visited Godfrey to offer him presents and pay homage to the new ruler of their land. They were shocked to find Godfrey in his tent, sitting on the ground, resting against a bale of straw. He had no guards, no crown, in fact none of the trappings the Arabs expected in a monarch. An interpreter explained their surprise to Godfrey.

Godfrey smiled. "There is no shame in a king or any other man sitting on the ground," he said. "It is where we all return in the end."

He was buried at the foot of Calvary—the hill where that other King had met death a thousand years before.

10

the king of jerusalem

The struggle for power in Jerusalem began immediately. Godfrey had named no successor and left no sons. By feudal custom, Godfrey's inheritance should fall to his nearest relatives, his brothers. But Eustace was in Europe, and Baldwin was far to the north, in Edessa. For several months there was no ruler in Jerusalem.

The Arabs, who had also heard of Godfrey's death, began raiding Christian villages and cutting up supply columns between Jaffa and Jerusalem. In Egypt, the vizier, still smarting after his defeat at Ascalon, began assembling an army.

Daimbert was content with the situation. He was helpless to stop the Arab raids, and he could not see in them a serious danger. His only concern was protecting his own position from his fellow Christians. He claimed that Godfrey had willed his title to the Church, but he could not produce a document to prove it. It is not likely that Godfrey's knights would have accepted the will, even if it had existed. Already they saw the kingdom tottering.

Some of Godfrey's men met secretly, and one of their number was sent north with a message for Baldwin. They urged the count to hurry to Jerusalem before Daimbert could blunder away the kingdom. Daimbert learned of the message and sent a letter of his own—to his old friend Bohemond. Daimbert asked Bohemond to intercept Baldwin on the road and detain him—kill him, if necessary. In return, Daimbert promised to support Bohemond in his own bid for the throne.

The letter was a mistake. Daimbert's messenger was captured near Tripoli by Raymond of Toulouse. Raymond read the letter and destroyed it. He was certainly not going to allow Bohemond, the man he hated above all others, to capture the crown and title that had been denied *him*. Besides, Raymond had nothing against Baldwin—the only leader of the crusade he had not quarreled with.

The letter would not have reached Bohemond in any case. In August, Bohemond had made his first mistake. With his own province fairly secure, Bohemond had ridden north that month to fight the Turks in the upper Euphrates Valley, north of Edessa. He had only three hundred knights and a handful of foot soldiers. His victories at Antioch and Dorylaeum had made him overconfident.

Bohemond wandered into a Turkish ambush, and his men were cut to pieces. The Danisment emir had his revenge. Bohemond was bound in chains and led off to a prison deep in the Taurus Mountains.

Barely a year after the fall of Jerusalem, all but two of the leaders of the Crusade were gone. Baldwin, strictly speaking, could not be counted as one of the leaders. He had taken part in none of the battles after Dorylaeum; his trip to Jerusalem was a hasty pilgrimage in fulfillment of his vows. And yet, a full year before Godfrey was elected ruler over Jerusalem and months before Bohemond had grasped the great prize of Antioch, Baldwin of Boulogne had become master of a territory as large as many kingdoms in Europe.

Baldwin had never made a secret of his ambitions, but he had lived all of his life in the shadow of his older brothers. The shadow chafed him. He had little interest in religion, and at thirty-three, his prospects seemed bleak. His early conquest of Tarsus was poor and liable to be claimed by the Byzantine emperor. He had found his wife and children dead. He had nothing more to lose. So while the main army was struggling over the passes of northern Syria in the fall of 1097, Baldwin had set his face to the east. With him, Baldwin took an Armenian mercenary named Bagrat, who told of a great city beyond the Euphrates.

Armenians had been moving into the Euphrates Valley for over a century. They were Christians who followed their own rite without direction from Rome or Constantinople. At the moment they had been temporarily subdued by the Turks—who were having trouble keeping down their unruly subjects. Bagrat convinced Baldwin that the Armenians were only waiting for a suitable man to appear and lead them in revolt.

Baldwin took 500 knights and 2,000 foot soldiers and set out toward Edessa. The Turkish garrison fled when the Crusaders approached. The Armenian prince of the city, an old man named Thoros, met Baldwin and clasped him with tears in his eyes.

Baldwin enjoyed a hero's welcome, but he soon made it clear that his services came with a price. Under pressure, Thoros adopted Baldwin as his son and named him his heir in a public ceremony. Thoros had never been popular with his people. By a not so strange coincidence, Thoros died a few days after the adoption—the victim of a rioting mob, which Baldwin could have broken up easily if he had wanted to. Baldwin's treachery against the old man was the first of a long series of actions that earned him the lasting hatred of the Armenians.

As soon as he was proclaimed count of Edessa, Baldwin threw out all Armenians who held high positions in the city and replaced them with his own knights. When there was a hint of treason whispered about his friend Bagrat, Baldwin had him thrown in prison and tortured. The new count systematically robbed the population, offering lands and money to any Frankish knight who would join him. In only one instance was he foiled. He announced his intention of marrying an Armenian girl, the daughter of one of the richest men in the country. After the ceremony, the bride's father fled the city, taking with him all of the promised dowry.

There is no question about Baldwin's ferocity. Within months he had driven the Turks from the country around Edessa, and when Kerbogha came to Edessa on his way to relieve Antioch, Baldwin inflicted crippling losses on the Turkish army. Because of Baldwin's action, Kerbogha wasted three precious weeks, and Bohemond had time to get inside Antioch and save the Crusade.

What is doubtful is the necessity of his repressive methods. Baldwin would have argued that the Armenians were uncertain subjects at best, and he was simply gathering his rightful spoils as a conqueror. But even William of Tyre, the Latin historian, conceded that Baldwin's rule in Edessa was harsh and brutal. The only thing Baldwin could not be accused of was religious persecution against the heretic Armenians. He simply had no interest in the subject.

By Christmas 1099, Baldwin felt secure enough to make the dangerous journey to Jerusalem. It was a happy reunion with Godfrey. The two brothers had never followed the usual feudal custom of fighting with each other. But Baldwin must have noticed the strain in Godfrey's face. It must have occurred to him that Godfrey could not live forever and that the kingdom of Jerusalem would one day be without a leader.

So Baldwin was ready. He received the news of his brother's death in October 1100 and set out immediately for Jerusalem. He left Edessa in the hands of his cousin, Baldwin of Le Bourg.

The journey to Jerusalem was perilous. The death of Godfrey and the capture of Bohemond had inspired the Muslims. The Egyptian army was on the way to Ascalon; Turks were raiding close to Antioch. Baldwin had to cross hundreds of miles of Muslim-occupied territory with only 160 knights and a few hundred foot soldiers for escort. The future of the whole crusading movement hung in the balance.

Baldwin's severest test came on a narrow mountain pass outside Beirut. Turks from Damascus had blocked the road along a steep ledge, and Baldwin was forced to withdraw to a plain between the mountain and the sea. The Turks foolishly followed Baldwin's retreat. Once on the flat ground, Baldwin ordered his men to wheel about. They broke the Turkish ranks in a headlong charge. The pass was opened.

Baldwin arrived at Jerusalem in November. With the handful of knights who had accompanied him and the men of Jerusalem, he marched toward Ascalon. The vizier had waited too long. The

Egyptian army would not come out of the fortress, and Baldwin returned to Jerusalem with a bloodless victory.

If there was any doubt about Baldwin's right to succeed to his brother's title, it was dispelled by his triumphant return. The people of Jerusalem thronged the streets to acclaim their new king. Only Daimbert and Tancred were unhappy. Tancred withdrew into Galilee, and Daimbert offered to make peace. Baldwin's coronation took place on Christmas day, 1100. Daimbert personally placed the golden crown on Baldwin's head.

Baldwin did not share his brother's scruples. He took the title of king, and he dressed and acted the part. It is said that he wore robes of spun gold and a turban like some sultan of the East. He rode abroad on a magnificent charger he had named Gazelle—and no horse could match him for speed or beauty. The Arabs were impressed. Here, surely, was a king.

Baldwin's kingdom, as he soon discovered, was a poor inheritance. South of Jerusalem the Dead Sea poked like a fat finger into bleak ranges of treeless mountains and desert where dust storms hung like mile-long veils across the caravan routes. To the west, the same storms made the port of Jaffa a death trap for ships in certain seasons. Only to the north in Galilee did the rich soil produce a harvest.

The Muslims controlled most of the country. The kingdom consisted of the single port, a few villages around Jerusalem and in Galilee, and the broken-down fortress of Ramla. The road connecting Jerusalem to Jaffa was a tenuous thread, constantly cut by bandits. Bedouin tribes from the desert east of the Jordan struck at travelers near Bethlehem. And the Egyptians, only temporarily cowed, still threatened from Ascalon.

Baldwin's biggest troubles were his lack of men and money and his isolation from the other Crusader states in the north. There was little he could do about the first. The second he solved by spreading fire and terror among the Bedouins. He filled his treasury with plunder from caravans, taking prisoners and giving them up for huge ransoms, and incidentally putting an end to attacks on pilgrims.

It was during an attack on a rich caravan on the east side of the

Jordan that Baldwin showed his chivalrous side. Baldwin and his men had surprised the Arabs in their camp where they had stopped for the night. Most of the Arab men were killed in their tents, and the women were taken captive, along with the herds and an immense treasure. The wife of the sheikh who had outfitted the caravan was among the captives. She was pregnant and ready to give birth. Baldwin learned of her condition and ordered her released with her servants. He left blankets, food, and two camels, then headed back toward Jerusalem. The woman gave birth by the side of the road and was found by her husband within a few hours. The sheikh swore he would repay Baldwin for his courteous gesture.

In May, Baldwin took Caesarea with the help of a fleet from Genoa and allowed another massacre to take place. He meant to show what would happen to any town that resisted him in the future. Then, in September, he heard of an Egyptian army moving up from Ascalon again.

The Crusaders were outnumbered more than ten to one when they caught up with the Egyptians at Ramla. Baldwin divided his men into two groups and sent the first on a desperate charge into the Egyptian ranks. The Crusaders were cut to pieces. The Egyptians, believing the Franks had been wiped out, hurried forward in disorder. With his second company of knights, Baldwin mounted his horse and led another charge. The Egyptians broke before him and scattered. Thousands of their number were killed.

The battle was a clear victory for the Franks, but half of Baldwin's force had been wiped out. When he rode back to Jerusalem, Baldwin knew he could not afford another such victory. The armies of Egypt would return; they could afford to throw away a few thousand men. Baldwin had barely two hundred to defend his capital.

Fortunately there was fresh news from Europe, and Baldwin had cause to rejoice, for it looked as if his manpower problem might be solved. The success of the first Crusade had touched off a storm of enthusiasm in Rome and all the cities of Europe. The second wave of the Crusade was setting forth.

The second wave began much like the first. Urban's successor, Pope Paschal II, preached a new Crusade in a number of European towns. Once again the great lords took up the cross, and their names read like an honor roll of European nobility—William of Aquitaine, Stephen of Burgundy, Conrad of Germany. Once again four separate armies set out across Hungary and Bulgaria and were met by Alexius at Constantinople. The largest and most fanatical of the four groups consisted of Lombards from Italy led by Anselm, the Archbishop of Milan. Conrad of Germany led another large force, which followed Peter the Hermit's winding route through the Danube region. The other two armies were much smaller, consisting of a few hundred French knights led in separate groups by those two strayers from the first Crusade, Hugh of Vermandois and Stephen of Blois.

The news of the capture of Jerusalem had come as a blow to Stephen. He had been publicly branded a coward and perjurer, but the public humiliation was nothing compared to the abuse heaped on him by his wife. To add to his troubles, the pope issued a decree declaring the deserters from Antioch excommunicated unless they returned to fulfill their vows. Sadly, Stephen took to the road in September 1100, his wife's words still ringing in his ears.

The Lombards and French under Stephen joined forces at Constantinople in April 1101. There they met a hero of the first Crusade who was languishing in the palace with little to do. He was Raymond of Toulouse. The new Crusaders begged him to lead them against the Turks.

Raymond had left Jerusalem after the battle of Ascalon and wandered north. He had not forgotten Tripoli, and for almost a year he had been in camp preparing for the siege that would occupy him for the rest of his life. In the fall of 1100 he had come with his wife and children to spend the winter with Alexius. It had been a pleasant few months, but Raymond was growing restless. The sight of the great new army acclaiming him as their leader stirred his pride. He agreed to take them to Jerusalem.

Raymond lost control of the army almost as soon as they were out of sight of Constantinople. The Lombards, who made up the majority, had a hero of their own to match the Frenchman, Raymond. They had come up with a fantastic scheme. They meant to rescue Bohemond from the Danisment emir.

The plan was madness. Raymond and Stephen of Blois argued hopelessly against it. They had experience with the Turks. They knew that an expedition across the Turkish homeland in the midst of summer was suicide. The Lombards stubbornly insisted, and they had their way.

For two months the army marched eastward across mountains and barren plateaus. Kilij Arslan retreated before them, devastating the countryside along their route. The Crusaders were harassed by small bands of Turks who hit them from the flanks and rear, then scuttled away before the Crusaders could retaliate. By the end of July the army was forced to move in tight formation without scouts or foragers. They resembled a herd of cattle driven ever eastward by the Turks. Raymond urged the army to turn north and break through to the Black Sea, where they could find Byzantine ships. The Lombards would not listen. They continued marching east until they reached a place called Merisvan (Merzifon). There the combined Turkish armies under Kilij Arslan and the Danisment emir were waiting.

The battle began with showers of arrows, which fell heaviest among the Lombards. They were struck with panic. Raymond tried to rally the men, but after a few moments he found himself practically alone on a small hill, surrounded by Turks. He would have been killed, but Stephen of Blois showed courage for once and cut his way through the Turks to rescue Raymond. Together they retreated to the camp, where the French and a group of Germans were holding fast. The first day of the battle ended with the fragmented Crusader army holding a thin line near the camp and the Turks surrounding them.

Raymond knew there was no hope. Under the cover of darkness he slipped from the camp with his bodyguard and rode hard for the coast. When the other leaders discovered that Raymond was gone, they too decided the time had come to leave. At dawn the army found itself with no leaders and the Turks closing in. The few men who had horses were the lucky ones. The foot soldiers, the women, and the children were left behind to be butchered.

The Turks fell on the camp and killed nearly everyone they found. Only a few of the prettier women were spared for the slave markets.

While Raymond's men were being massacred, the other two armies were crossing the Bosporus and marching south. The first got as far as Heraclea, where they ran into the Turks, fresh from their victory over Raymond. The Crusaders were ambushed and wiped out almost to the last man. Conrad of Germany was one of the few to escape. The last of the armies, with Hugh of Vermandois, met the same fate a few days later. Hugh was badly wounded in the battle, and though he managed to escape with a few of his men, he died within two weeks. He was buried at Tarsus.

Raymond, Stephen of Blois, and the other survivors assembled at Constantinople, where they were bitterly reproached by Alexius. Raymond in particular was disgraced. It was difficult to accuse the old veteran of cowardice, considering his past record, but he was certainly guilty of stupidity and ineffectual leadership. By one of those strange quirks of history, though, the ultimate blame was not laid on Raymond or the Lombards. The people of Europe could not believe one of their own had caused the disaster. They had to have another scapegoat. The rumor was circulated that Alexius had deliberately sent the Crusaders into the mountains to be massacred—and for hundreds of years the name of Alexius was synonymous with treachery.

Raymond left Constantinople by sea and landed at Antioch at the beginning of 1102. There he was arrested and handed over to Tancred. It was Raymond's final humiliation.

Stephen of Blois, Conrad of Germany, and the handful of others boarded ships for Jerusalem, where King Baldwin eagerly awaited the expected reinforcements.

11

the triumph of the cross

King Baldwin learned of the disaster at Mersivan long before the survivors straggled into his domains. There was nothing to be done about it; Baldwin was not the type to brood over failure. So in the early spring he sent a detachment of men north to Beirut to welcome the visitors and escort them to Jerusalem. The time for Easter was approaching. Stephen, Conrad, and the others would at least have the consolation of celebrating the season in the holy places.

The visitors stayed for nearly a month. They were joined by the thousands of native Christians who thronged the city during Holy Week. They walked in the processions to the Church of the Holy Sepulcher, and they listened as the patriarch recounted the story of the miracle that had occurred in that place a thousand years before. They fulfilled their vows, and perhaps there was consolation for them. But they lingered too long.

Spring softened the harsh country around Jerusalem. The winter rains dried, and fresh breezes sprang up along the coast. One of those breezes carried William of Aquitaine safely to St. Symeon in the latter part of April. Stephen of Blois was anxious to follow. But Stephen's ill luck continued to plague him. A few days after William's departure, Stephen boarded a ship at Jaffa. He had barely cleared the port when a storm struck, driving his ship aground. Stephen emerged from the sea and returned to Jerusalem. There was no hope of finding another ship. The pilgrim fleet from Genoa was not due for another month.

Stephen returned to find Baldwin and the court stirring with preparations for battle. A fresh army from Egypt had been reported landing at Ascalon. Advance parties were already moving toward Ramla. Baldwin was not worried. The ships which had taken William of Aquitaine back to St. Symeon had unloaded several hundred men, and they were standing by at Jaffa. More were gathering in Galilee. Baldwin explained the situation to his visitors.

Conrad of Germany and Stephen of Burgundy joined Baldwin eagerly. They were anxious to wipe out the humiliation of their flight from Merisvan. Stephen of Blois had no choice but to follow their example.

According to the reports, the Egyptian force moving on Ramla was only a small raiding party. Baldwin decided the best course was to take his own force, about two hundred knights and several hundred foot soldiers, to dispose of the raiders. He would leave his reserves to handle the main Egyptian army. Only Stephen of Blois objected to the plan. He distrusted the reports. Surely, he argued, the Egyptians would not be so foolish as to send a raiding party against Ramla when they had been so badly defeated only a few months before.

Stephen's objections were ignored. His reputation as a coward had destroyed his credibility. Baldwin rode out of Jerusalem with his two hundred knights, and Stephen joined them. The army rode into the plain between Jerusalem and Ramla full of confidence.

For once Baldwin's spies had failed him. On the afternoon of May 17, the Crusaders spotted the Egyptian army. It was no small raiding force that confronted them. The Egyptian ranks seemed endless. In fact, there were over 20,000 horsemen—some of whom were already circling to cut off the Crusaders' retreat. Baldwin drew his sword and spoke urgently to his men. "By God's grace we may break through them and escape the battle if we stay together."

They had no choice. The Crusaders drew up in a tight line and charged. Under the first shock the Egyptians gave way. But they re-formed quickly, and the battle swirled across the plain. A handful of knights escaped and fled toward Jerusalem. Baldwin kept his small group together and cut his way through to the fortress at Ramla. There they barricaded themselves behind the walls and managed to fend off the Egyptians until nightfall.

The Arabs would not attack at night, but they surrounded the fortress. The Crusaders could see their fires dotting the plain around Ramla, and they knew that when the battle resumed in the morning, none of them would survive. The walls of Ramla were in sad shape; only one tower was in good repair. Baldwin, Conrad, and Stephen of Blois crowded into the tower to pass a sleepless night.

No record of their conversation that night has come down to us, but it is known that sometime during the night an Arab visitor slipped over the walls and called out Baldwin's name. The startled Crusaders dragged the Arab into the tower and demanded to know what he wanted. The Arab explained that he was a sheikh of a tribe from the east side of the Jordan. The previous year Baldwin had attacked his caravan.

Baldwin impatiently ordered him to come to the point.

"My wife was ready to give birth. Because of your mercy, my wife and my son live. I have come to repay the favor."

The Arab offered to lead Baldwin through the Egyptian lines and guide him to safety.

It was a desperate chance. The Crusaders discussed the situation. Only one or two men would have a chance of getting through. One of them had to be Baldwin. Without him, the kingdom would crumble under the Egyptian attack. No one would accuse him of deserting his comrades under the circumstances.

Baldwin agreed. With his squire, one man-at-arms, and the Arab sheikh, Baldwin slipped out of the fortress. They muffled their horses and made their way cautiously past the Egyptian camp. Within an hour the lights of the camp fires were behind them.

At dawn, the Egyptians closed in on the fortress. They

swarmed over the walls and dragged wood against the tower. Torches were thrust into the wood, which turned into an inferno. Rather than burn, the Crusaders gathered themselves for one last charge on foot. They broke from the tower, screaming their battle cry. Most were cut down at once. Conrad of Germany fought until he was literally buried under the press. He was driven to the ground and taken captive. A few of his men survived with him to be taken back to Cairo. Stephen of Blois was killed. The news of his death gladdened his family; he had finally redeemed himself by his heroic action.

Baldwin spent three perilous days roaming the countryside, while the Egyptians scoured the land, hunting for him. They were furious when they found he had escaped. All the men who had accompanied Baldwin were killed in the flight. Only the swiftness of Gazelle saved the king.

He arrived at Arsuf (Arsur) north of Jaffa, which was on the point of surrendering, and rallied the men. Then he called for food and drink and promptly went to sleep. "For a king," a chronicler wrote, "also has need of that."

Baldwin's escape had been a miracle. Within a few days he was at Jaffa, where the army rallied to his side. They were joined by reinforcements—pilgrims who had put in at the port. Baldwin sent a hurried message to Tancred. It was time to forget past differences. The kingdom was threatened.

Amazingly, the Egyptians had not taken the opportunity to march on Jerusalem, which was defenseless. They paid for their mistake. On May 27, Baldwin led his reconstructed army against them. Inspired by the king and the True Cross, which was carried at the head of the battle by Bishop Gerard, the Crusaders fell on the Egyptians and routed them.

The second battle of Ramla proved once and for all that the Crusaders had come to stay. It was Baldwin's finest moment. The Egyptians retreated to Ascalon, and did not threaten the kingdom again. Baldwin would spend the remaining years of his reign fighting one battle after another. But it would be many decades before a Muslim army would advance on the walls of Jerusalem, and the men inside would despair for the death of their king.

While Baldwin was hanging grimly on to Jerusalem, that other landless adventurer, Tancred, was busy in the north. Tancred had been called to Antioch shortly after Baldwin's coronation to take Bohemond's place while he was in captivity. Tancred soon proved himself an able ruler. He strengthened the defenses of the city and pushed the Muslims almost to the walls of Aleppo. By 1103, Antioch was the richest and most secure of the Crusader provinces. Not even Alexius, who was still determined to regain his property, dared threaten it.

Tancred was happy in Antioch, and in no hurry to see his uncle return. Unfortunately for Tancred, however, Bohemond in captivity was only a little less dangerous than Bohemond free. Bohemond's stay in prison had not softened his personality or blunted his cunning. He had been released from his dungeon shortly after his capture and lived under a kind of house arrest at the court of the Danisment emir. He had made many friends during his three years in captivity, including members of the emir's own family. So Bohemond was well informed of the negotiations that were going on about his release.

The person most interested in Bohemond was Alexius Comnenus. The emperor had offered a staggering sum for Bohemond's ransom—260,000 gold pieces. The Crusaders could not hope to raise that kind of money, especially since Tancred refused to contribute. The emir was on the point of accepting Alexius' offer when his old enemy and sometime ally, Kilij Arslan, heard of it. Kilij Arslan demanded half of any ransom be paid to him, since he was overlord of the Turks. The Danisment emir was naturally offended by the demand and by Kilij Arslan's pretensions. The negotiations with Alexius broke down, and there was nearly war between the two Muslim rulers.

Then Bohemond spoke up in his own cause. He knew that if Alexius got hold of him, he would never again see the light of day. So Bohemond offered the Danisment emir a smaller ransom—one he would not have to share—and an alliance against Kilij Arslan. The emir was intrigued by the offer. As usual, the Muslims were more concerned with their own squabbles than with presenting a united front against the Crusaders. The emir accepted, and in the spring of 1103, Bohemond was released.

Bohemond's reunion with Tancred was strained, but there were no reprisals. Bohemond probably considered that in Tancred's place he would have done the same thing. Bohemond took over the principality of Antioch once again, and immediately organized an expedition against the Byzantine city of Marash, far to the north. With the Turks allied with Bohemond, the city had no choice but to surrender. Alexius was in a rage, but for the moment he was helpless.

Bohemond was not content with grabbing distant pieces of Byzantine territory. He meant to bring the Byzantine emperor to his knees. In 1104, he restored the regency of Antioch to Tancred, and departed for Europe in a search for more men.

Bohemond spent three years visiting European capitals. Pope Paschal listened sympathetically to Bohemond's complaints against the Byzantine emperor. Bohemond blamed Alexius for the disaster at Mersivan, and hinted darkly that the real enemy of the Latin Church was not the Muslims but the Greeks. In 1106, he was at the court of King Philip of France. The French king was so impressed by Bohemond that he offered one of his daughters in marriage to Bohemond and another to Tancred. The marriage of Bohemond to Constance of France took place in the spring of 1106. Bohemond took his new wife to Sicily, stayed just long enough to see her safely pregnant, and then took his new army on a campaign against the Byzantine Empire.

Bohemond's scheme was hopeless from the start. He had no regular navy, and despite his successes in diplomacy in the French capital, he was short of men. He landed on the western coast of Macedonia in the autumn of 1107, and laid siege to the Byzantine fortress of Durazzo (Durrës).

Alexius had not been idle during Bohemond's absence. The emperor had signed a treaty with Kilij Arslan to offset Bohemond's alliance with the Danisments, then set about reinforcing his western provinces. Alexius allowed Bohemond to land on the peninsula, then sent his navy to cut off the Norman's supply routes. Within a few days after his landing, Bohemond discovered that he was the one under siege, cut off by the fortress in front and the blockaded port in the rear. Alexius allowed Bohemond to sit for months, while disease and famine gradually decimated his army. By September 1108, Bohemond was ready to surrender.

It was a humiliating meeting for the former prince of Antioch. Alexius had drawn up an agreement, which was read to Bohemond. Bohemond was to apologize publicly and formally for his past misdeeds and agree to become the vassal of the emperor. In return, Alexius would allow Bohemond to rule Antioch as his representative. Any of Bohemond's followers who would not acknowledge the emperor as their ruler were to be removed by force.

Bohemond signed the agreement, but he did not return to Antioch. He knew that Tancred would not stand for it, and his own prestige had been destroyed forever. He could not challenge the emperor again. Bohemond returned to Italy, where he died quietly three years later, leaving two small sons.

As for Tancred, he rejected the agreement out of hand. Alexius was the ruler of Antioch on paper. On paper it would remain.

12

the full tide

The last of the Crusader states was a long time being born. Raymond of Toulouse had suffered one defeat after another, first at the hands of his fellow Crusaders and then from the Turks of Asia Minor. His arrest by Tancred on a charge of "betraying Christendom by his shameful desertion at Merisvan" had been the worst and final blow.

It must have amused Tancred to have the old count in his power and under arrest on such a cynical charge. Tancred was not concerned with Christendom; he was concerned only with Tancred. Raymond, as a friend of Byzantium, was still a threat. By humiliating him and by extracting a strong oath in which Raymond promised never to attack any fortress or town in the territory of Antioch, Tancred neutralized that threat. Raymond was released a few weeks after his arrest. He gathered his remaining men and marched away from Tancred and Antioch forever.

To an observer it must have seemed that Raymond was finished. Some of his friends urged him to return to Toulouse. He was nearing his seventieth year; he had abandoned wealth and position. He had a wife and infant son, and no inheritance to leave them—no inheritance but his dream.

It was a persistent dream. The city of Tripoli was one of the most beautiful in Lebanon. Olive groves and green orchards dotted the land inside the walls. To the east the mountains with their cool pine and cedar forests guarded the fertile plain. It was a dream worthy of a count of Toulouse.

Raymond had only three hundred men when he took up the siege of Tripoli once again in 1102. It seems like an impossibly small number, but Raymond's three hundred were no ordinary soldiers. They had been selected by that most impartial and most ruthless of tests for the elite. They were survivors.

In 1102, an army of several thousand men set out from Damascus to push them into the sea. They were joined by Arabs from Tripoli and from fortresses in the mountains. There were four armies in all, and they outnumbered Raymond's men by more than twenty to one.

An Arab historian, Ibn al-Athir, recorded the result. Raymond divided his men into four groups—two of a hundred each, and two of fifty. The Turks from Damascus found their ranks shattered in the first charge, and they fled the field. Raymond then swung his whole force against the Arabs of Tripoli, who had been holding against one of the groups of fifty. The Arabs were slaughtered by the hundreds, and survivors limped back to the city. It was an incredible feat, and the Arabs acknowledged it. Raymond of Toulouse was becoming a legend as famous among the Arabs as Bohemond and Baldwin of Jerusalem.

Fame would not dent the walls of Tripoli, though, and Raymond's three hundred men were not enough to try an assault. In the year 1103, Raymond ordered a castle built on a hill overlooking the city. The castle was completed the following summer and christened Mount Pilgrim. It became Raymond's headquarters for a permanent siege. Soon other buildings sprang up around the castle, and a small town with markets, churches, and homes faced Tripoli.

The town was constantly plagued by fire and by raids. In the latter part of 1104, a Muslim raiding party slipped out of the city and set fire to some buildings near the castle. Raymond directed the fire fighting himself. He climbed to the roof of a burning building and shouted orders to his men, who warned him in turn that the fire was spreading. It was too late. The roof collapsed, and Raymond went down in the blaze. He was rescued, but he never recovered from his wounds. He clung to life for three months and died in his castle in February 1105. His body was taken to Jerusalem and laid beside Godfrey.

Tripoli held out for four more years. There was some argument about Raymond's inheritance during that time. Raymond had left his oldest son, Bertrand of Toulouse, to govern his lands in France, and an infant, Alfonso-Jordan, in Mount Pilgrim. After ten years, Raymond's wife had decided she had done enough crusading. She was anxious to return to France with her infant son. So an exchange was made. Bertrand came east, and the young Alfonso went home to Toulouse. The trouble arose because a regent had been appointed after Raymond's death. William-Jordan, Raymond's cousin, had fought beside the old count in every engagement. He understood the problems the Crusaders faced in their new country, and for four years, until Bertrand arrived, he had tightened the siege around Tripoli. He felt, when Alfonso left, that the inheritance should go to him.

Bertrand arrived in early 1109, with 4,000 horsemen and a fleet of ships under his command. It was a staggering force. William-Jordan appealed to Tancred in Antioch for help. Tancred was all too willing to meddle, especially since he saw an advantage for himself. William-Jordan offered to become Tancred's vassal.

The news of the squabble alarmed King Baldwin of Jerusalem, and he rode north in June 1109 with five hundred knights. Instead of fighting, however, he summoned Tancred, Bertrand, and William-Jordan to a court. They were joined by Baldwin II of Edessa, so the full might of the crusading forces was gathered before Tripoli. The royal court decided that the two disputants must divide Tripoli between them. Bertrand would rule the city itself, and William-Jordan the surrounding towns and fortresses. On the death of either man, the whole country would fall to the survivor. William-Jordan became Tancred's vassal, and Bertrand became the vassal of Baldwin.

With the dispute settled, the combined armies turned their attention to the city. Tripoli put up a token resistance, but on July 12 surrendered peacefully to the Franks. Any Muslims who wished were allowed to leave the city with all their property. The rest became subjects of Bertrand, the new count of Tripoli.

Within a few days, Bertrand became sole ruler. William-Jordan was killed by a shaft from a crossbow when he tried to stop an argument between two men-at-arms. No one seemed to know who had fired the shot. There were whispers of murder, but nothing could be proved.

Baldwin's diplomatic success in Tripoli was both a sign and a beginning. It was a sign that the king of Jerusalem must eventually become the moral and legal head of all the Crusader states. Even Tancred had been forced to accept the decision of the royal court. And it was the beginning of the final formation of the kingdom. Acre had fallen in 1104, the Egyptians had been turned back from Ramla for the third time in 1105, and the land borders in Galilee and along the Jordan desert were being fortified by a strong chain of fortresses. Only the coastal cities of Tyre, Sidon, and Beirut still held out.

The capture of Acre had been a giant step. Its harbor was sheltered from the prevailing north wind, which had wrecked so many ships at Jaffa. The stream of pilgrims setting out from Europe could count on a secure harbor, and trading ships from Genoa, Venice, and Pisa increased their fortunes. The Italian fleets were important, not only because they carried men and supplies to the impoverished kingdom, but because they neutralized the Muslim navy. A fleet from Genoa had formed the last link in the blockade around Tripoli, and in 1110, when Baldwin brought his forces in front of Beirut, it was a Pisan squadron that cut off the sea approaches. Bertrand of Tripoli obligingly added his own men to the siege. Beirut held out a mere three months, then surrendered under the usual terms.

Baldwin's capture of Beirut had barely been completed when he met one of the most extraordinary pilgrims ever to visit his kingdom. He was the first of the kings of Europe to come to the Holy Land, and he brought with him a fleet of high-prowed ships that had once been a symbol of pagan terror to the coastal towns of Europe. He was the Viking, Sigurd of Norway.

Sigurd's voyage had begun three years before. He had visited England, then stopped in Portugal and Spain to fight the Muslims of those countries. Roger of Sicily had welcomed and feasted him, then sent the Vikings on to their final destination at Acre. Baldwin personally met the Viking king and escorted him to Jerusalem. The two kings were instant friends. Sigurd asked Baldwin to name any city on the coast, and the Viking would take it for him. Baldwin named Sidon.

The Vikings swarmed to their task, and in December 1110, Sidon became the next city to fall to the kingdom of Jerusalem. Sigurd sailed away into song and legend with the other epic Viking seafarers, and reached home after an absence of nearly ten years.

Baldwin's attempt to capture Tyre ended in failure, but the city was effectively neutralized. With the coast fairly secure, Baldwin turned his attention to the south. He ordered construction of a great castle south and east of the Dead Sea. When the castle was completed a few years later, it became known as the Krak de Montreal (Ash Shawbak)—the Royal Mountain. It was an immense citadel, capable of housing several hundred knights and their horses and withstanding siege for months at a time. It was the first, but far from the mightiest, of the castles the Crusaders would build over the years to guard their borders.

From the site of Montreal, Baldwin drove south to the Gulf of Aqaba at the tip of the Red Sea. The move created a wedge between the Fatimids of Egypt and the rest of the Muslim world. Trade caravans now had to pass through Baldwin's territory at every point and were subject either to raids or heavy taxes.

In 1112, Baldwin was relieved of his last rival among the Franks. Tancred was only thirty-six and had survived countless battles, but he was struck down by a raging fever that might have been typhoid. There were no medicines to fight the disease, and Tancred knew he was dying. He called his followers to his bedside and gave instructions concerning his will. He had no children, so he turned over the government of Antioch to his nephew Roger of Salerno. He made one provision. Bohemond's young son was still living in Italy. Roger had to promise that if Bohemond II ever came to Antioch, the country would be turned over to him. Tancred's last request was that his wife, Cecilia of France, marry the son of Bertrand of Tripoli.

Tancred's death and the marriage of Cecilia to Pons of Tripoli meant that the entire Frankish community was related to Baldwin by marriage or vows of fealty. It must have given the old king (for Baldwin was now past fifty) a sense of security and power far beyond anything he could have dreamed of when he fought his way from Edessa to Jerusalem a dozen years before.

Baldwin was tireless. For six years after Tancred's death, he fought continuous battles, riding to aid Baldwin of Edessa on one occasion and Roger of Antioch on another. In 1115, he entered into the strangest alliance of all, when the sultan of Iran marched west to unify the Muslims under his own rule. The Muslim ruler of Damascus was not anxious to be unified and appealed to the Franks for help. The three provinces of Antioch, Tripoli, and Jerusalem all provided troops. The sultan was thoroughly defeated, and Damascus remained independent.

The alliance was proof that conditions were changing dramatically. What had started out as a religious war was turning into a fight for political survival. The change was inevitable. The religious fervor that brought pilgrims from the West did not sustain them long in the East. Those who came to fight and survived usually went home after a few months. The permanent residents knew that a strong, unified Muslim attack would mean the end for them. It is due to Baldwin's insight as much as his sword arm that the attack never came. Baldwin ultimately reached a precarious understanding with his enemy. It was an understanding based on mutual hatred, and there was constant warfare, but there was no longer any thought of extermination. For the Franks, it would have been impossible. For the Muslims, it would have been costly and dangerous. Only a *jihad*, or holy war, as in the days of Muhammad and Omar, could have united the Muslims. None of the Muslim princes were willing to give up their independence.

By 1118, Baldwin felt strong enough to launch his most ambitious attack ever. With only two hundred knights and four hundred foot soldiers he marched south, intending to invade Egypt. He had no hope of defeating the whole country, of course. The attack was really a large-scale raid in reprisal for Egyptian raids across the borders. The surprised Muslims fled from their outlying fortresses, and by the end of March, the Crusaders had reached the Nile.

It was Baldwin's last triumph. In the Nile delta, the king felt the pain from an old wound suddenly flare up again, and he ordered his men to begin the long march back to Jerusalem. It soon became obvious that Baldwin was dying. He was carried on a litter as far as the fortress of el-Arish in the Sinai desert. He died there, held like a child in the arms of the bishop of Ramla.

Baldwin's body was carried back to Jerusalem, and he was buried on Palm Sunday next to his brother Godfrey. It is said that even the Muslims grieved over the death of the king. A few months later, in Constantinople, that other great emperor, Alexius, also died. With the passing of those two men, the first phase of the Crusades was ended.

part two

Beyond the sea

13

OUTREMER

We who were Westerners have become Orientals. The men of
Italy and France have become men of Galilee and Palestine. He
who was a citizen of Rheims or Chartres is now a citizen of Tyre or
Antioch. We have already forgotten the land of our birth. . . .

Some of us have married a Syrian or Armenian, some even a
baptized Saracen; then he has a whole new family. We speak the
languages of the country, and trust has brought us together. The
immigrant has become a native.

These words were written about the year 1125 by Fulcher of
Chartres, a French priest who had accompanied Robert of Normandy on the first Crusade, then remained in Jerusalem to write
one of the most important chronicles of the time. Fulcher was
nearing the end of his life. He has seen the Crusade transformed
from a wild dream proposed by Urban at Clermont into a struggling but viable state in Palestine. He had stood at Dorylaeum
while Bohemond rallied his men in the face of the Turks howling
around them. He had gone with Baldwin on the treacherous
journey from Edessa to Jerusalem, and he had witnessed
Baldwin's triumphant return from Ramla.

Now Fulcher could afford to be optimistic. A new generation of

Crusaders had come from Europe and settled alongside the sons of the first Crusaders—sons who had been born and grew up in Palestine. Baldwin of Le Bourg, the last of the knights who had ventured across the sea in 1096, ruled in Jerusalem as Baldwin II. The old divisions were gone. Bohemond II of Antioch and Count Pons of Tripoli were joined to Baldwin's family by marriage. A cousin, Joscelin of Courtenay, ruled in Edessa. All acknowledged Baldwin as their overlord. The Crusaders had a new name for their united country. They called it Outremer—Beyond the Sea.

Outremer, as Fulcher described it, was a unique blend of strange alliances and bitter warfare, religious fervor and tolerance, Western government and Eastern customs. When the first Crusaders set out from Europe, they may have dreamed of a Western kingdom transplanted whole to the eastern shores of the Mediterranean, but in fact that was impossible. After their first victories, they had found themselves a ruling minority in a country whose people far outnumbered them, and who had long established customs of their own. Like many conquerors before them, they were seduced.

The Franks may have been superior in battle—the Muslims freely acknowledged that—but the Muslims had by far the superior culture. The Franks had lived in drafty, smoke-filled castles that reeked of sweat, manure, and the blood of slaughtered animals. Rushes spread over stone or dirt floors made their beds. Their food was bland and coarse. When they came to Outremer, they found marble palaces decorated with bright carpets and draperies. They discovered spices, feather beds and cushions, and the curious custom of taking regular baths. European medicine was crude and ineffective; the Arab doctors could cure wounds that in Europe would mean a prolonged, agonizing death. It is small wonder that the Franks adopted a new way of life. The result was often a shock to Europeans who came to Outremer as pilgrims.

A pilgrim landing at Jaffa or Acre in the year 1125 might well wonder at the sights and sounds that greeted him. He would be met by a knight of one of the military orders—the Templars or Hospitalers—and guided to one of the many pilgrim inns. Along the way he would pass crowded marketplaces where people of six different cultures shouted at each other in a common language. He might see a European nobleman dressed in a loose robe and turban, and his wife beside him draped in silk and veiled like an Arab woman. If that was not enough of a shock, he might turn a corner and see a group of Arabs peacefully entering a mosque, and from a minaret high above hear a muezzin calling the faithful to prayer.

After the massacre in Jerusalem, the Muslims had fled the countryside, but after twenty-five years, those who were willing to live under Frankish rule were being permitted to move back. They worshiped freely at their mosques, paid the Frankish taxes, and brought their disputes to the Frankish courts, where they usually found satisfactory justice. The Arabs of Syria and Egypt were properly horrified by those who "collaborated with the enemy," but privately admitted that the poorer people were often better off under Frankish rule than they had been under the Muslim governors.

All was not peace and brotherhood, however. Baldwin II was not the equal of the first Baldwin in ferocity or stature, but he continued Baldwin's policy. This meant constant war along the borders. In 1124, Tyre, the last of the coastal cities in Muslim hands, surrendered. A year prior to that, both Baldwin II and Joscelin of Courtenay had been captured by Turks near Edessa, and the king of Jerusalem was forced to pay a huge ransom for his release. The ransom had been raised by attacking the Turks in Syria to pay the Turks in Edessa.

With all his wars, Baldwin II faced much the same problem as Baldwin I—a shortage of man power. There were many knights in Europe during those years who came to Outremer to serve the king of Jerusalem for a time, but they usually went home after a few weeks. What was needed was a strong permanent force. The answer came in the year 1118, when a French knight named Hugh of Payens came to the king and asked permission for him and his eight companions to found a brotherhood for the protection of pilgrims. The king gave Hugh a house connected to the royal palace on the site of what had once been the Temple of Solomon. The brotherhood soon took the name "Templars."

The Templars combined the two strongest ideals of the

Crusaders. They were both a military and a religious order. The members were all monks, who had taken the usual vows of chastity, poverty, and obedience, but they were also knights. At first their main job was to act as a kind of military police, guarding the pilgrim roads. They soon joined the king in his wars along the borders, where they distinguished themselves by always being first in the battle line.

The Templars were joined in 1119 by a second order of knights, the Hospitalers. The origins of the Hospital actually extended back to 1070, almost thirty years before the first Crusaders came to Jerusalem. In those days, when a journey to Jerusalem was an almost impossible hardship, a monk named Brother Gerard founded a small hospital to minister to sick and dying pilgrims who came to the Holy City. The Hospital had remained a purely charitable order for almost fifty years. Godfrey of Bouillon had donated land for the hospital building near the Church of St. John. In 1108 the Order of St. John was recognized by the pope as a legal order of the Church. Both men and women joined the Hospital and swore to devote the remainder of their lives to the service of poor and sick pilgrims. By 1119, it was apparent that the greatest need of the pilgrims was protection from Bedouin tribes. In spite of Baldwin's best efforts, the Arabs of the desert had proved too elusive to be disposed of for good. The monks of the Hospital buckled on swords.

The military orders had a strong appeal to men who felt the urge to take the cross but were shocked by the easy life and the changes taking place in the Crusader kingdoms. A knight of the Temple or Hospital was bound by vows of eternal poverty and could probably look forward to death at the hands of the infidel. But death in the service of God was glorious martyrdom, they believed, and carried the sure promise of Heaven.

There were two side effects. As with any close-knit, exclusive body, a feeling of smugness soon appeared among the members of the orders. They wore distinctive uniforms to set themselves apart from ordinary knights—a red cross on a white tunic for the Templars and a white cross on a black tunic for the Hospitalers. They lived together in stark surroundings, sleeping on stone floors, keeping strict silence at meals, and were forbidden to hunt

any animal except the lion. It is no wonder, in an age when the
service of God was the highest ideal, that the military orders
became as famous for their arrogance as for their courage in battle.

The second effect was sometimes tragic. A strong rivalry
evolved between the two orders, which eventually led to outright
hatred. In battle, each tried to prove itself more fearless than the
other. That made them an almost invincible force, since they were
never allowed to surrender and, if captured, were never ransomed, but it sometimes led to serious tactical blunders.

The king of Jerusalem was thus reinforced by two strong military arms, which he could usually count on in times of serious
crisis. The trouble was they were not tied directly to the king.
Their suzerain was the pope, and they took orders only from the
head of their order, the Grand Master. In later years, when the
strength and independence of the orders grew until they were
nearly the equal of the king himself, this would have serious
repercussions.

The other important source of manpower came from the
independent city-states of Italy. The republics of Genoa, Pisa,
and Venice all depended on trade for their livelihood, and all kept
strong fleets of warships. In the early days of the Crusade, ships
from Genoa had provided critical aid during the siege of
Jerusalem. A Pisan fleet had cut off Beirut, and Venetians had
blockaded Tyre. The Italians were well paid for their services. In
most cases they received blocks of land in the towns they helped
capture and a virtual monopoly on trade. The trade they developed enriched Europe with spices, silks, ivory, and gold. It also
enriched Italy with new ideas, which would eventually flower
into the Renaissance.

Like the military orders, the Italian cities were fierce rivals and
could never be counted on to cooperate with each other. In a
sense, this was good for the Crusaders, since the competition
made each of the cities eager to aid the Franks in their fight against
the Muslims—always in return for large concessions. The Italians' greatest rival was Constantinople. Sea power had ended
Bohemond's dream of conquering the Byzantine empire, and the
Italians knew that sea power would someday be the key to unlock
the treasure chests of Constantinople. In the meantime, they

waited, and the growth of their power steadily weakened the great city on the Bosporus.

Inevitably there was some friction between the Crusaders and the Italians. From the beginning, the men who settled in Palestine were mostly French, and they had nothing but contempt for the Italians. As a result, the Italians stayed mostly in the coastal towns, insulated and independent. If they had ever had any enthusiasm for the Crusade as a religious venture, they quickly lost it in the face of the Franks' overwhelming snobbery.

For their part, the Muslims were continually amazed at the actions of the Franks—rude barbarians who had appeared suddenly in their midst. The Muslim attitude is best summed up in the tales of an Arab historian and traveler who was born in the early part of the twelfth century and spent most of his life fighting and living among the Franks. His name was Usama ibn Mundiqh. Usama's book, which is a kind of travelogue and autobiography, shows the Franks as crude, unpredictable, and occasionally amusing. He admits their ferocity in battle, but dismisses their prowess as "the virtues of animals."

The thing that shocked the Muslims the most was the casual attitude the Franks held toward women. Not only did women go abroad with their faces uncovered, they actually visited and talked on the street with men who were not their husbands. From our viewpoint such laxity is hardly shocking, but to a Muslim of the time it was proof that the Franks were totally without honor or jealousy.

The independence of the Frankish women is demonstrated by the story of a girl taken captive by Usama's father and given to the emir of a Muslim town in Syria as a gesture of friendship. The girl was both young and beautiful, and her new master fell in love with her. She gave him a son, and the emir made the boy his heir. When the emir died a few years later, both the boy and his mother had risen to a position of wealth and power. But the boy's mother had never forgotten her own people, and one day she escaped and made her way back to the country of the Franks. Usama reports in astonishment that though the boy continued to rule over his father's town, his mother happily settled in with the Franks and married a cobbler. Usama concludes that the Franks are a race cursed by God, who would never marry with another people.

At the same time, however, Usama tells of a Frankish knight with whom he made friends. The Frank was returning to Europe and offered to take Usama's son with him, to increase his education and teach him the science of chivalry. Usama was horrified. He would rather, he relates, see his son living in a dungeon than among the Franks in Europe. Usama made polite excuses and declined the offer. It is clear that Usama is suffering from double standards. True, the Franks rarely married Muslims, but their objections were religious rather than racial. It was religion that divided the two sides most deeply.

On one occasion, Usama tells us, he visited the Temple at Jerusalem (apparently during a truce) and the hour for prayer came. He knelt facing Mecca and was in the midst of his prayers when a Frank rushed forward and wrenched him around to the east. The Frank was terribly upset. "This is the way to pray," he insisted. The Templars pulled the Frank away and apologized to Usama. A few moments later, the same Frank rushed in again, and the performance was repeated. The Templars threw the man outside this time. "He has just come from the West," the Templars explained. "He has never seen anyone pray facing Mecca."

Usama went outside, where he saw "what a twisted face that devil had, and how he was shaking and unnerved by the sight of someone praying toward Mecca."

14

the tide turns

Baldwin II of Jerusalem reigned for thirteen years. They were years of consolidation and defense rather than expansion. The first Baldwin had pushed the borders of the kingdom to their limit. It was all Baldwin II could do to hold on to them.

Egypt remained quiet during those years, but the Turks were stirring in the north, threatening Antioch and Edessa. By the ninth year of Baldwin's reign a new power had risen in Syria. His man was Imad ed-Din Zengi. Zengi had been appointed the governor of Mosul in 1127 and had immediately drawn the independent city of Aleppo into his domain. Zengi moved carefully, well aware of the fate that had befallen the men who attempted to unite Muslim Syria in the past. He knew that his most formidable enemies were the Franks and the Muslims of Damascus. In 1128 he arranged a two-year truce with Joscelin of Edessa and spent the time strengthening his holdings.

In the meantime, Baldwin II turned his attention to a pressing problem at home, hardly aware of the new threat growing in the north. Baldwin had four daughters by his Armenian wife, but no sons. In 1126, he was feeling the effects of age. He knew it was time to find husbands for his daughters and arrange for the succession.

That same year, a young man growing up in Italy came of age and left his birthplace to lay claim to his inheritance in the East. He was Bohemond II. Young Bohemond was not an attractive character. He suffered from conceit, and he had none of his father's patience or cunning. He had been raised on tales about his father, who had become a legend in Italy, and he arrived in Antioch with a single burning ambition—to kill every Turk he could lay his hands on. Instead of the Turks, however, his first quarrel came with his neighbor to the north, Joscelin of Edessa. The reasons for the quarrel are not clear (apparently Bohemond demanded the old count pay homage to him—an insult beyond bearing), but the results were nearly tragic. Joscelin made war on Antioch, and only the intervention of Baldwin stopped the bloodshed.

It was clear that the young Norman was not the man to inherit Baldwin's kingdom, but Baldwin did want to strengthen his ties with Antioch. So he offered his second daughter, Alice, in marriage to Bohemond. The wedding took place in the latter part of 1126. Within a year a daughter, Constance, was born in Antioch.

Baldwin's oldest daughter, Melisinde, was the heir to the throne of Jerusalem, and Baldwin cast about for a suitable husband for her. There was no one in the country worthy of the honor, so the king sent messengers to the king of France, asking him to nominate someone. The king settled on one of his most powerful vassals, Fulk the count of Anjou.

Fulk of Anjou was forty years old, rich, and a veteran of countless wars. He was well liked and seemed a perfect choice. Only Melisinde was not thrilled. The count was too old for her. Melisinde's objections were ignored, and she was married on June 2, 1129. Melisinde was soon pregnant, and Baldwin lived long enough to see that he had a grandson. The succession was safe.

In Antioch, Alice was unhappy with her new husband. He was gone most of the time, fighting Turks along his borders. Bohemond's overwhelming desire to live up to his father's name made him hated by the Turks and feared by his own men. On one occasion Bohemond captured a castle formerly belonging to the province of Antioch and now held by the Turks. He took several prisoners, and instead of ransoming them (the usual practice), he killed them all on the spot. "This," he said smugly, "is the way to make war on Turks."

Usama tells of a meeting with Bohemond. The Norman came riding into the territory of Usama's father, with several of his men behind him. Bohemond challenged every Turk he met to single combat. When a group of Turks rode out from the city, Bohemond charged them alone. His horse was killed, and he fought his way out on foot. "You," he shouted to his men, who had not had time to come to his rescue, "are no better than women."

That kind of insult and Bohemond's foolhardy valor soon cost him his life. In February 1130, Bohemond rode into Armenia and was met by a large army headed by the Danisment emir. The encounter was a complete surprise to both sides. Neither had expected to meet the other. Bohemond was hopelessly outnumbered, but he chose to fight. His men were slaughtered, and Bohemond went down with them. Once again, Antioch was without a ruler.

More precisely, the new ruler of Antioch was the two-year-old girl, Constance. As Bohemond's wife, Alice had no legal rights. Baldwin II was forced to ride to Antioch at the request of the barons and settle matters. He was met by a complete surprise.

Alice was not ready to give up her power. She assembled men loyal to her, slammed shut the gates of the city, and prepared to resist her father. She even sent a message to Aleppo, offering an alliance with the Turk, Zengi, if he would help her. The messenger was intercepted by Baldwin, who was naturally enraged by his daughter's rebellion. With a large force of knights, Baldwin marched on the city.

The people of Antioch were not prepared for a civil war. They opened the gates, and Baldwin entered the city without a fight. Alice was hiding in the citadel, and offered to make peace when she saw that all was lost. Her father generously agreed and forgave her, but the rebel was sent to Latakia, where it was hoped she would live quietly and repent her sins. It was an unfounded hope.

Baldwin II died on August 21, 1131, and the crown passed to Fulk of Anjou. King Fulk was a worthy successor to Baldwin, but he had two weaknesses. He was not well known, and he was very much in love with his wife, Melisinde. Baldwin was followed in death by Joscelin of Edessa. His son, Joscelin II, was, like Alice, half Armenian. He had no love for the king of Jerusalem. As soon as he was crowned, Fulk found himself with a large-scale rebellion on his hands.

The plot centered around Alice, who had returned to Antioch. Joscelin II was prepared to support her in a war against the king. When Fulk met the challenge by marching toward Antioch, he discovered that Pons of Tripoli had thrown in his lot with the rebels. Count Pons refused permission for the king to cross his territory.

Fulk took ship at Beirut and landed at St. Symeon. He was attacked by Pons, but the count had underestimated the king's power. Pons was defeated, and most of his men were taken prisoner. The Turks, delighted by the sight of the Franks fighting each other, decided to take advantage of the situation. They attacked the weakened county of Tripoli. Pons, who had escaped the first battle, suddenly found himself bottled up in his castle by the Turks.

There was something comic in the situation, but Fulk realized this was no time to gloat. He released the prisoners, and the whole Frankish army set out to rescue Pons. The count gave up all thought of rebellion after that. Once the Turks were defeated, he swore loyalty to the king. Joscelin II soon followed. Alice was foiled again.

The rebellions were clear signs that the Frankish kingdom was beginning to crack. True, King Fulk had proved that a strong, determined leader could hold them together, but it was a patch-work arrangement. The tide was turning.

Fortunately for the Franks, the Muslims were deeply divided during the next several years by rebellions and assassinations in the distant courts of Baghdad and Cairo. The caliph of Baghdad went to war with the sultan, and Zengi was occupied by the conflict for many years.

Fulk finally settled the problem of Antioch by bringing in

another French baron, Raymond of Poitiers, to marry the young heiress, Constance. The girl was only ten years old, but the situation in Antioch had deteriorated too far to let the matter go any longer. The Turks had captured a number of border fortresses and were hammering at the borders of Tripoli as well. By 1137, Zengi had turned his attention once again to the Franks. Count Pons of Tripoli was killed that year by the army of Damascus, and Fulk was defeated by Zengi in a battle at Montferrand (modern Ba 'Rin, about twenty miles inland between Tripoli and Latakia). Fulk escaped with his life, but one of the most important fortresses in Antioch was lost forever.

In the midst of all this trouble, Fulk was suddenly confronted by a new menace. John Comnenus, the emperor of Byzantium, was well aware of the Frankish troubles in Antioch. He was ready to assert his father's old claim to the city. In the spring of 1137, the emperor arrived at Antioch at the head of a large army. Raymond of Antioch had no thought of resistance. He was new to the country. He asked King Fulk for advice. Fulk was resigned. He advised Raymond to surrender, and the emperor ran up the flag of Byzantium over the citadel in Antioch.

Actually the intervention of John was a good thing for the Franks. Raymond was required to swear loyalty to the emperor, but he remained prince of Antioch. More importantly, the emperor was ready to take the field against Zengi. In the end, John's expedition accomplished little, but it gave the Franks time. John failed to take Aleppo or any other major Muslim town, but Zengi was halted in his raids against the Franks. For the next five years, things were relatively peaceful. Fulk made an alliance with Damascus, which was still independent of Zengi, and spent his time in his own kingdom, directing the building of new castles. In 1140 the mighty Kerak of Moab (Al Karak), which the Muslims called the Stone of the Desert, was completed. The defense of the castles passed into the hands of the military orders, and the pilgrims to Jerusalem found safety at last.

Then, near the end of 1143, an unforeseen tragedy occurred. King Fulk and his wife were on a picnic near Acre when a rabbit jumped out of the brush and scurried away. Like a small boy, the king happily spurred his horse in pursuit of the rabbit. The horse stumbled; the king was thrown. He died of his injuries on November 10, and the kingdom was thrown into a panic. Fulk had two sons. Baldwin, the elder, was thirteen. Amalric was only seven.

It was the moment Zengi had been waiting for.

The death of Fulk split the old cracks among the northern Franks wide open. Raymond of Antioch was soon quarreling with Joscelin of Edessa. The boy king and his mother were helpless to heal the trouble, and Zengi struck swiftly. He chose Edessa because it was the most advanced and most exposed of all the Frankish territories. Joscelin was in his second city, Turbessel, when Zengi appeared outside Edessa with siege engines and battering rams. The count was not too concerned. The walls of Edessa were thick. They would keep Zengi out.

They did—for twenty-eight days. Edessa fell on Christmas day, 1144, and the panic in the city led to a massacre. Thousands of citizens of Edessa were killed before order was restored. The surviving Franks were executed by Zengi without mercy. The Armenians found themselves subjects of the Turks once more, after nearly fifty years of Frankish rule.

In Turbessel, Joscelin was stunned by the turn of events. Bitterly he blamed Raymond of Antioch for his troubles. Raymond had refused to go to the aid of Edessa, and the army of Jerusalem had arrived too late. But Antioch was in danger too. Raymond finally awoke to the common danger. He appealed to Constantinople.

John Comnenus' son, Manuel, had become the emperor of Byzantium in 1143 on the death of his father. He might have been willing to go to the aid of Edessa, but he was engaged in his own wars with the Turks. For the moment he could do nothing. Zengi backed off a little at the threat of Byzantine intervention, however. After the fall of Edessa, he turned to the one Muslim city in Syria that still resisted him—Damascus.

Then the Franks were treated to an incredible stroke of luck. During the siege of Damascus, Zengi discovered one of his servants stealing wine from one of his cups. Zengi angrily rebuked the servant, and that night, while Zengi was sleeping in his tent, the servant slipped in and murdered him. The siege of Damascus

broke up, and Zengi's two sons began fighting over his inheritance. The unified Muslims fell apart.

Zengi's death meant the immediate danger for the Franks was
over, but it did not restore Edessa. The armies of Palestine were
too weak to attempt a reconquest, and the Byzantines were unwilling or unable to help. The only remaining course was to appeal to
the pope, and the men who had taken it in the first place—the
barons of Europe.

The loss of Edessa was a serious blow to the Church. The
Church had not forgotten its possessions in the East, although it
had often been distracted by troubles of its own. In 1144, the pope
was Eugenius III, a man who was on fairly good terms with the
most powerful kings of Europe, Louis VII of France and Conrad
III of Germany. Eugenius could not travel to France himself, but
he persuaded one of the most famous churchmen of the day to
preach a new crusade. He was Bernard of Clairvaux, later to be
canonized as Saint Bernard.

Most people in Europe were not too enthusiastic about a
crusade. They had not forgotten the disaster of 1101 at Merisvan.
But Bernard was the most eloquent speaker of his time, and he
could sway crowds. Symbolically, he made his first call at Clermont, where Urban had electrified the people fifty years before.
The response to Bernard's speech was overwhelming. Thousands
hurried forward to take the cross. Among the first was King Louis
of France.

It was extraordinary that a king of France should go on a
crusade. Nothing like it had ever happened before. Bernard was
only beginning, though. In the fall of 1146, he traveled to Germany and met with Conrad. The Germans had not exactly
glorified themselves in the first Crusade, and Conrad received
Bernard coolly. Bernard struck at the king's conscience, and spoke
as if he were Christ making the appeal: "What more could I have
done for you that has not been done?" Conrad was moved. He
agreed to go.

The armies gathered. By June 1147, Conrad was making his
way through Hungary. Louis of France was about a month behind. With Louis went his fiery young wife, Eleanor of

Aquitaine. They followed the route of the first Crusade to Constantinople, where Emperor Manuel was horrified at their numbers. He sent the Crusaders on their way as soon as possible.

The Crusaders may have remembered the disaster of 1101, but
they soon proved they had learned nothing from it. They marched
from Nicaea to Dorylaeum instead of taking the longer but safer
coast road, and they carried few provisions. Conrad's army
reached Dorylaeum on October 25, exhausted by their long
march. There they found a host of Seljuk Turks waiting for them.
The situation was almost the same as the first battle of
Dorylaeum, but the Germans had no Bohemond to lead them.
Conrad tried hopelessly to keep his men together, but they
panicked. By nightfall, Conrad had lost most of his army. The
survivors fled toward Nicaea, where they joined King Louis.

The French treated the German survivors with utter contempt.
They had no desire to share their fate, however, and Louis decided to take the coast road south. Conrad's remnant marched in
the rear. The French soon found themselves harassed by bands of
Turks along their flanks and in their rear. By the time they
reached Antioch, in the middle of March 1148, the army was
thoroughly demoralized, and the French and Germans had become bitter enemies.

At Antioch, they found new troubles. King Louis was anxious
to march on to Jerusalem, but Raymond urged the king to join him
in an attack on Aleppo, where Zengi's son, Nur-ed-Din, ruled.
To further his cause, Raymond sought the support of the king's
wife, and that proved his undoing.

Eleanor was not in love with her husband. She was young and
self-willed, and Louis was an aging bore as far as she was concerned, "more like a monk than a king." She began casting amor-
ous glances at Raymond. There were whispers of scandal. To
crown it all, Eleanor demanded a divorce. Louis was furious. He
would never support Raymond's war now. Louis and his army left
for Jerusalem, where the young king, Baldwin III, and his mother
were engaged in a struggle of their own.

Baldwin III was eighteen years old and had not yet been
crowned. All power rested in his mother's hands as regent.
Baldwin was sincerely devoted to his mother, but she had little

political sense, and the barons of Jerusalem were restless. They had divided into two factions. Louis VII of France and Conrad of Germany stepped into the middle of this brawl, and for the moment the problem was diverted. The first question that had to be settled was the direction the new Crusade was to take.

A great assembly was held at Acre, with all the barons of the kingdom, the Grand Masters of the military orders, and the leaders of the new Crusade attending. The discussions went on for hours. All thought of retaking Edessa had disappeared. Finally a decision was reached. The combined armies would move on Damascus.

A more foolhardy plan could not have been conceived. Not only was Damascus an ally against Zengi, and now Nur-ed-Din, it was practically impregnable. Nevertheless, the Crusaders began their siege of the city of July 24. The emir of Damascus had no choice but to request aid from his old enemy, Nur-ed-Din.

The siege of Damascus lasted five days. There was almost no cooperation between the factions of the army. Thirst and blistering heat sapped morale. By the twenty-eighth, Nur-ed-Din's forces were approaching. The Franks of Jerusalem finally realized their mistake. The army broke up and returned to Jerusalem.

The second Crusade had been a fiasco from beginning to end. The only thing it accomplished was the divorce of Eleanor and Louis, which would have terrible consequences for France, and the strengthening of Nur-ed-Din, which would have worse consequences for the kingdom of Jerusalem.

15

the LURE of egypt

The dismal failure of the second Crusade finally shocked the
Franks of Tripoli, Antioch, and Jerusalem into reality. They
knew, from the moment of their retreat from Damascus, that they
were men apart. No more massive help from Europe would be
coming to Outremer. If they were to survive, they must do it
alone, and they must unite.

There were a few more convulsions. King Louis lingered
pointlessly at Jerusalem for another year and sailed for home in the
summer of 1149 with tears in his eyes. Even as he was sailing,
Raymond of Antioch was marching toward Nur-ed-Din and
Aleppo on a virtual suicide mission. He had only a few hundred
knights to throw against Nur-ed-Din's thousands, and it is clear
that Raymond had no intention of returning. In the battle that
followed, Raymond's army was wiped out completely. The
prince of Antioch fought to the last. "He made a clear space
around him with his sword," says the historian William of Tyre.
He died with his sword in his hand.

It is hard to understand Raymond's motives. Perhaps he
blamed himself for the failure of the Crusade and wished to offer
this last spectacular gesture as an act of penance. Or perhaps he

123

believed a miracle would come, and he would be hailed as the savior of the kingdom. In the end, his death accomplished nothing. His title passed to his five-year-old son, Bohemond III, and Constance became regent of Antioch.

With Raymond gone, and much of the country around Antioch under his control, Nur-ed-Din turned to finish off Joscelin. The end came for the count in the summer of 1150. He was captured by Nur-ed-Din's Turkish mercenaries, blinded, and sent off to a prison in Aleppo. He died in captivity nine years later.

The disappearance of Raymond and Joscelin accomplished what the threat of extinction and the promise of the second Crusade could not. It united the Franks under the head of the king of Jerusalem. Nur-ed-Din discovered that the real prize, the focus of the holy war for the Muslims, was still too strong. Al-Quds must remain in the hands of the infidel a little longer.

Nur-ed-Din did not attempt to finish off the Franks. After capturing Joscelin and extinguishing the remaining Christian holdings in Edessa, Nur-ed-Din was required to settle accounts with Damascus. The city had broken its alliance with him as soon as the danger was passed, and made a new alliance with Jerusalem. For the next four years, Nur-ed-Din would be occupied with civil war.

In Jerusalem, Baldwin III was growing into a king. He was well past the age when he should have been crowned, and his mother should have retired from the regency. But like her sister Alice, Melisinde loved power and did not part with it easily. Baldwin's advisers urged him into a showdown with his mother, who insisted on being crowned queen with her son and dividing the kingdom with him. The idea appalled the barons of Jerusalem. They needed a single leader capable of pulling them together in battle and in the council. They secretly arranged to have Baldwin crowned alone. The unwilling patriach of Jerusalem, who was one of Melisinde's supporters, yielded at the point of a sword. The crown was placed on Baldwin's head. When Melisinde learned of the coronation, she locked herself in the citadel of Jerusalem and declared war on her son.

There was no war. Melisinde's supporters melted away, and

she was forced to surrender within a few days. Baldwin, who was an easygoing man, took no further action against her. Melisinde retired to her home in the country. From then on, she devoted most of her time and intrigues to the Church.

Baldwin soon proved himself as capable as his father. A year after he was crowned, while Nur-ed-Din was still at Damascus, Baldwin began the long-postponed siege of Ascalon. It was a formidable task. The Egyptians had fortified the town for years. In 1153, it was one of the strongest fortresses in Muslim hands, bristling with towers and high walls. On the seaward side, the city closed around an excellent harbor, where Egyptian ships brought in a steady flow of supplies. The Egyptians were proud of their fortress. They had named her the Bride of Syria.

The siege lasted for seven months. The Franks were unable to undermine the walls, and they would not push their towers close enough to gain a foothold. By July they were discouraged enough to think of calling off the siege. But then they had a stroke of luck. An immense tower, which the Franks had spent weeks building, was pushed against the walls. From the top of the tower, the Franks could shower arrows and fire into the streets of the city itself. The Egyptian garrison retaliated by slipping out of the city one night and setting fire to the tower. The tower and the wall turned into an inferno. The heat split the stones of the wall, and a huge section toppled into the dust.

A band of Templars were the first to react. They poured through the breach and into the city. Then the Templars decided the honor of taking the town should go to them alone. A few Templars guarded the hole in the wall to keep any other Franks from entering, and the rest rampaged through the streets. But they were too few. The Egyptians counterattacked, and every one of the Templars was killed. The breach was blocked up.

But the incident had scared the Egyptians. They reflected that an honorable surrender was more sensible than an assault and probable massacre. Baldwin agreed to their terms, and the Muslim citizens of Ascalon were permitted to leave with all their belongings. After the long string of failures in the north, the capture of Ascalon restored some of the confidence and shaky prestige of the Franks. It was hoped by some that it was a sign of a new beginning. Baldwin III was promising to become the equal of the first Baldwin.

Baldwin was not finished with the northern provinces, however. There still remained a piece of unfinished business. Since Raymond's death, Antioch had been in the hands of a woman and a small boy. It was time for Constance to remarry. Constance was in no hurry about it. She rejected a long string of suitors, and Baldwin, who had been nearly helpless in the face of one woman, was not the man to force Constance into marriage. Baldwin had left Constance to her own devices while he directed the siege of Ascalon, and in the spring of 1153, Constance made her choice.

The Crusades had always attracted a fair share of madmen, adventurers, and fanatics to their ranks. But the name that stands out among all the rest, the name that became a curse among the Franks for as long as they remained in Palestine, was that of the man Constance chose to marry. He was Reynald of Chatillon.

At first the objections to Reynald were purely snobbish. He had no noble blood or riches or prestige. He was a landless knight who had come with Louis VII on the second Crusade, and stayed because he had no prospects at home. Reynald was handsome, and he charmed Constance with his attentions. The young princess (she had been widowed at twenty-two) fell in love. The marriage was arranged in the spring of 1153, when Constance was twenty-six.

Baldwin was happy to be relieved of Antioch. Manuel Comnenus, who was still technically suzerain over Antioch, was not. He disliked Reynald and distrusted him. Nevertheless, Reynald made an alliance with the emperor and rode off to the first duty of a prince of Antioch—subduing the Turks. Reynald's greatest friends were the Templars, who saw in the dark knight a man after their own heart. He was ruthless in battle and took lives as carelessly as he took food and drink.

In 1156, the rift between Reynald and Manuel Comnenus exploded. Reynald was always short of money. The Turkish invasions had left Antioch a poor province. The only way he could restore his treasury was to take it from someone else. Reynald's eye lit on the rich, peaceful Byzantine island of Cyprus.

Reynald's invasion of Cyprus in the spring of 1156 was so brutal and savage that even the hardened Franks were shocked by it. For three weeks Reynald's men roamed over the island, raping, burning, and killing. Manuel's nephew, John Comnenus, was taken prisoner. Churches were destroyed, crops were rooted out and burned, herds were rounded up and driven to the sea. No one was spared. Old men and children had their throats cut. Priests were mutilated. Finally, with Cyprus a smoking ruin, Reynald returned to Antioch.

Manuel was helpless to avenge the pillage for nearly two years. In 1158, he secretly met with ambassadors sent by King Baldwin, who was as anxious to humiliate Reynald as the emperor was. The ambassadors discussed an alliance with Jerusalem and the possibility of a marriage between Baldwin and Manuel's niece, Theodora. In the fall of the year, Manuel secretly moved south at the head of the Byzantine army. He was assured of Baldwin's cooperation, and no word of his approach leaked out. His coming was a complete surprise to Reynald. At Antioch, the terrified Reynald put up no resistance. The city surrendered without a fight. In a meeting with the emperor, Reynald was forced to lie in the dust and proclaim his repentance. The emperor spared his life, but Reynald had to turn over the citadel to the Byzantines and promise never to attack Byzantine territory again.

The Franks were relieved of Reynald two years later. He was captured by Nur-ed-Din during a raid near the Euphrates and imprisoned at Aleppo. But Reynald was not finished. He endured his captivity, spent his time learning Arabic, and waited. He would have to wait nearly sixteen years, and then he would emerge to play his role in the last act.

Nur-ed-Din continued his steady progress, taking Damascus in 1154. He now ruled all of Syria, but the Seljuks of Asia Minor and the Fatimids of Egypt remained his enemies. He dreamed of conquering these last two pockets of resistance and then turning the full might of Islam against the Franks. In 1156, he made a truce with Baldwin, and directed a war against the Seljuks as his first step. For a few years there was relative peace in Outremer.

Baldwin married Theodora Comnena in 1158, ensuring close ties between the Byzantines and the Franks during his reign. The king was growing increasingly popular, and he settled down to a rule which even the Muslims described as marked with justice and wisdom. It was a short-lived rule. In 1162, Nur-ed-Din received unexpected news. Baldwin III was dead.

The king had shown no signs of ill health, but disease was rampant in the country. There was some talk of poison, but no one could conceive of a motive for such an act. Even the Arabs joined in mourning for the king. Nur-ed-Din's advisers suggested that Baldwin's death gave them a perfect opportunity to attack the Franks, but the emir replied, "I cannot attack people mourning the loss of so great a ruler." It was a rare compliment from a Muslim to a Frank, and the opportunity passed. Baldwin's brother, Amalric, became king.

Amalric was not as personally popular as Baldwin. But he was no weakling, and no one thought to revolt against him, which was the usual practice in the Crusader states. The only difficulty raised was over his wife, Agnes of Courtenay, the daughter of Joscelin II of Edessa. Agnes had made herself despised among the barons of Jerusalem by developing a reputation for unchastity. She was supposed to have had several lovers before her marriage to Amalric, and some whispered that she had not given up all of them after her marriage. Perhaps the rumors were true. In any case, Amalric agreed easily enough to divorce his wife before he was crowned. He only insisted that his two children, Sibylla and Baldwin IV, be recognized as legitimate.

Amalric was a farsighted man, and he realized that Baldwin's policy of keeping peace with Nur-ed-Din while harassing the Egyptians was the key to Frankish survival. Nur-ed-Din was growing old and had spent much of his energy in a futile war against the Seljuks. But Amalric was not content with simply holding his own. He dreamed of restoring the glory of the first kings of Jerusalem and extending their conquests. So Amalric gathered his forces and the scene shifted.

In the year 1168, Egypt sprawled at the base of the Nile, fat and rich like a fruit that has gone unpicked and ripened too long. On the outside it was still a kingdom of wealth and splendor, but inside it was riddled with corruption. Since the fall of Ascalon, the Egyptian court had been weakened by a series of palace revolutions and assassinations. The caliph was only a figurehead; the real power lay in the hands of the vizier, a scheming man named Shawar, who had clung to power by a series of remarkable alliances.

In 1163, Shawar had been ejected from Cairo by a revolution. He had made his way to Damascus, where he appealed to the Syrian sultan, Nur-ed-Din, for help. The sultan sent his army under the command of his favorite general and friend, Shirkuh, to Cairo. With Shirkuh's help, Shawar was quickly restored to power, but he soon discovered the Syrians were more enemies than friends. Shirkuh refused to leave Egypt. With his army to back him up, Shirkuh began levying taxes, plundering the treasury, and genèrally behaving like a conqueror instead of an ally.

Shawar was not the type to suffer this abuse in silence. After a few months he sent ambassadors to the Franks in Jerusalem and offered an alliance against the Syrians. King Amalric was delighted, but the price he demanded was steep—a payment of 100,000 gold pieces a year. Shawar agreed, and in the summer of 1164, the Franks marched south. Shirkuh fled at their approach.

Shawar twice saved himself from Syrian invasion with Amalric's help. Amalric should have been content with the situation. His money problems were solved; the Egyptians were practically his vassals; the Muslims were so deeply divided that they were not a serious threat to the kingdom. The complicated political game had worked for four years, but Egypt's wealth and apparent helplessness were a great temptation. In 1168, Amalric made an alliance with the Byzantine emperor and launched an invasion of Egypt.

Shawar was enraged by this betrayal by his former friend—though it was just one more example of political backstabbing, which the Muslims had perfected. Amalric offered to call off his invasion in return for a payment of two million gold pieces. Shawar refused to submit to this robbery. The wheels had turned again. Shawar called on the Syrians and Nur-ed-Din for aid.

Nur-ed-Din was thoroughly fed up with Shawar and the whole problem of Egypt. Nur-ed-Din was a devout Sunnite Muslim. He hated the Shiite heresy almost as much as he hated the Franks, and he saw in Egypt's troubles a way to rid himself of both. In the fall of 1168, Shirkuh returned to Egypt to attack the Franks outside Cairo. With Shirkuh went his nephew, a young man who had already attracted attention for his valor in the wars against the Seljuks and for his devotion to the cause of Islam.

With his nephew's help, Shirkuh drove the Franks from Egypt, and Shawar soon discovered that he had made a terrible mistake. He was arrested by his liberators and summarily relieved of his head. Amalric was horrified at the results of his rash invasion. Not only had he lost his tribute, but Nur-ed-Din had suddenly united the two halves of the Muslim world as well.

It was a precarious union. The people of Egypt were still Shiites and hostile to the Syrians. It would take many months of careful maneuvering to consolidate the takeover. A few weeks after Shawar's execution, Shirkuh also died, from choking on a piece of meat he swallowed during a feast celebrating his triumphs. His nephew took his place as vizier of Egypt.

The nephew's name was Saladin.

16

the leper king

From the cluster of towers on Jerusalem's citadel, where he spent many hours walking and thinking, King Amalric had a panoramic view of his kingdom. The breeze that played over the heights gave him relief from the sweltering heat in the city. And each time he climbed the tower steps he was reminded of the mission that had brought his ancestors beyond the sea. To the east he could see the Church of the Holy Sepulcher. To the south ran the winding road to Bethlehem. And to the southwest, the hills of Judaea rolled away to the sea and the desert marches that separated his kingdom from Egypt. He knew that desert well now. He burned with shame at the memory of the humiliation he had suffered and the long retreat from Cairo. He meant to avenge that humiliation.

Amalric knew that he faced the greatest threat to the kingdom since the days when Baldwin I escaped alone from Ramla with the Arab host at his heels. Jerusalem had certainly been saved by a miracle then. There was always hope. Saladin clung to Egypt by his fingernails. Nur-ed-Din was an old man who must die soon. Death had always meant the breakup of empires in the past. Perhaps again . . . Amalric pushed the pieces of the political

131

chessboard around in his mind. Wistfully he contemplated an alliance with Saladin against the old man. There were rumors of a growing rift between them.

But the problems of Cairo faded in comparison with the black news Amalric had received from his friend and adviser, William of Tyre. As he walked over the dusty pavement stones of the tower that evening in the year 1170, Amalric grieved for his son.

Baldwin IV was a handsome boy. He had a quick intelligence that sometimes astonished his teachers. William had remarked that the boy could ride a horse like a man, although he was barely nine years old. And he had been provided the best tutors in the kingdom, including the future archbishop and historian, William of Tyre. "He never forgot an insult or a kindness," William wrote of Baldwin. "We were as careful about perfecting his character as we were about teaching him literature."

Sometime in 1170, when Baldwin was nine years old, William watched as Baldwin played with the other children in the court-yard of the palace in Jerusalem. They played a rough game, pinching each other on the arm to see which of them could endure the pain the longest. Baldwin never flinched. Curious, William called the boy to his side and asked to look at his arm. At first he thought Baldwin's immunity to pain was just one more example of courage. He soon discovered, though, that Baldwin had no feeling in his arm. Doctors were called to examine him. The truth became apparent. "We realized—and wept when we spoke of it—that the boy had leprosy."

Leprosy was a common disease in the East, and the Franks had strict laws to deal with it. A leper was almost a criminal. Lepers were not allowed to associate with other people, and they were shut up in bleak colonies where they were left to fend for them-selves and die. In fact, a leper was considered legally dead the moment his condition was discovered. He was a walking corpse.

Amalric would not allow this to happen to his son. In an age that was stark and unsentimental, there is no doubt of Amalric's love for the boy. He insisted that the barons recognize Baldwin as his legal heir. There was really little chance, it seemed, that Baldwin would ever become king. He could not live more than a few years. He could never marry. Amalric was only thirty and in excellent health.

Over the next four years Baldwin's disease progressed steadily. By the time he was thirteen it had begun to show in patches on his face and hands. The once-handsome prince became an object of pity and disgust to those around him.

By 1174, Saladin had secured his hold on Egypt. The Fatimid caliph was dead. The Shiites had been ruthlessly suppressed. And in May came news of the death of Nur-ed-Din. The emir's heir was another child, only eleven years old. Nur-ed-Din's empire began to fall apart. It was time for Saladin to gather the forces of Islam under his own rule.

Amalric moved to check the growing threat. In July, he made an alliance with the Syrian regents in Aleppo, who were fearful of Saladin, then began preparing an expedition. Within a few days, however, he was forced to take to his bed with a severe attack of dysentery. He died suddenly on July 11.

Baldwin the Leper was crowned king four days after his father's death. It was generally understood that Baldwin's reign was a temporary measure. Despite Amalric's insistence, the feeling was that Baldwin was already dead. Immediately the intrigues of the court began swirling around him. The prize was the crown of Jerusalem, which must pass to one of Baldwin's two sisters as soon as he was buried. Amalric's oldest daughter was Sibylla, fourteen years old and ready to be married. Isabella, the daughter of Amalric's second marriage, to Maria Comnena, was only two. Sibylla was the logical choice, but Isabella's supporters raised the ugly problem of the divorce. Sibylla was technically illegitimate, no matter what Amalric had said.

The court divided into two bitterly opposed factions. Agnes of Courtenay returned to court to protect her children's rights. She had not changed during her absence. As Amalric's wife she had been the target of gossip. As the king's mother, she was the subject of open scandal. She joined the petty intrigues with relish, sharing her bed with a number of men she found politically useful. The only good thing she brought to Jerusalem was affection for a dying boy, who desperately needed it.

Out of the confusion, Raymond III of Tripoli was appointed regent until the king became old enough to govern himself. Another tough old warrior, Humphrey of Toron, became commander of the army. Neither of these men was anxious to take sides in the vicious family feud splitting the kingdom, but they could scarcely ignore it. Raymond became the prime target for the hatred of the men around Agnes. Ultimately he was forced to side with Maria and the Princess Isabella.

While the Franks were busy in Jerusalem, plotting among themselves, Saladin was taking advantage of the opportunity to pick up the pieces of Nur-ed-Din's empire. Damascus welcomed Saladin as a conquering king. One by one the other Syrian cities fell under his control. The only resistance he met was at Aleppo, where Nur-ed-Din's eleven-year-old son resided. The citizens fortified their defenses and sent messengers to Jerusalem begging for help.

Raymond responded at once. The army of Jerusalem did not dare attack Saladin directly. Instead, Raymond chose to lay siege to the city of Homs (Hims). Saladin could not ignore the threat to his rear. He abandoned the attack on Aleppo and hurried south. Raymond slipped away. He had accomplished his task. Aleppo was still independent.

The Turkish regent of Aleppo was so grateful to the Franks that he released all the Frankish prisoners in his jails. Among them was Reynald of Chatillon, the dark prince who had ravaged Cyprus so many years before. Reynald's wife was dead, and he had no claims at Antioch, so he traveled to Jerusalem. There he joined in the feud. Agnes had found her strongest supporter. Reynald soon married the widow of the man who had commanded the great castle in the desert known as Kerak. Overnight he had become one of the most powerful men in the kingdom.

Baldwin was aware of the feud, and aware of the fate that awaited him. But if he was considered dead by his family and the court, he stubbornly refused to lie down. Children matured quickly in those days, and Baldwin was forced to grow up even earlier than most. At the age of fourteen, he suddenly made his voice heard. Under his mother's influence, Baldwin announced that the time had come to find a husband for Sibylla. The man he selected was William Longsword, a cousin of Louis VII of France. William was a wise choice. He was rich, a fearless knight, and he was related to the most powerful lords of Europe. Even Sibylla was happy. They were married a few days after William's arrival in Jerusalem, in October 1176.

The problem of the succession seemed settled. Within eight months, it was thrown wide open again. William was dead of malaria, and Sibylla was pregnant. The old quarrels flared up, more bitter than before. The Templars joined with Agnes, and the Hospitalers sided with Maria Comnena. The dispute over the succession was aggravated by the military situation, which was growing steadily worse.

In the fall of 1176, the Franks' last hope of support against Saladin was wrenched from under them. Manuel Comnenus had thrown away the entire Byzantine army in a poorly planned expedition against the Seljuk Turks. It could not have come at a worse time. Saladin was in Egypt, gathering men to eliminate the troublesome Franks once and for all. As soon as he learned of the Byzantine defeat, which even the emperor compared to Manzikert, a hundred years before, Saladin stepped up his preparations.

Then Baldwin showed his true stature. After William Longsword's death, Baldwin dissolved the regency. He was king, and he meant to rule. Raymond bowed to his wishes and retired. In the fall of 1177, he left Jerusalem for Antioch, where the Turks were threatening. Humphrey of Toron was ill with malaria. Sixteen-year-old Baldwin ruled alone. Saladin chose the moment to strike.

From Egypt, Saladin's 20,000 men marched up through Sinai toward Ascalon. Baldwin gathered every available knight in the kingdom and hurried to defend the fortress. Eighty Templars were at Gaza. Baldwin's force numbered about five hundred. Baldwin reached Ascalon just a few hours before Saladin.

Saladin left a small force to keep the king locked up at Ascalon. With the main army, he turned toward Jerusalem. There was no one to stop him. Baldwin realized the danger. He managed to send a message to the Templars at Gaza and told them to join him at Ascalon. When the Templars arrived, the king and his knights broke out of the fortress and rode hard up the coast.

Saladin had made a terrible mistake. His troops marched carelessly, with little order. Several hundred men had broken off from the main body to forage in the countryside. On November 25, the Muslim army was crossing a ravine just south of Ramla, at a place called Montisgard (between Ramla and Ibelin). There was some trouble with the baggage wagons. No one expected an attack.

Then, out of nowhere, it seemed, a line of Frankish knights led by a boy and a priest, who held aloft the case holding the fragment of the True Cross, swept down on them. Baldwin had circled to cut off the Muslim army from the north. The Franks attacked with almost inhuman ferocity. The front ranks of the Muslims were annihilated in the first charge. Baldwin threw himself into the thickest part of the fighting. The Egyptians panicked. Saladin's personal bodyguard was killed almost to the last man before Saladin made his escape. The army he had set out with was no more.

The Battle of Montisgard was an incredible victory, and the sixteen-year-old Leper King had saved Jerusalem. But in the end, the situation for the Franks remained desperate. For the next three years no one questioned Baldwin's right or ability to rule. He continued to battle with Saladin, but there were no decisive victories on either side. In 1179, Saladin nearly accomplished his task when he ambushed the tiny army of Jerusalem near the Sea of Galilee. Humphrey of Toron led a heroic, suicidal defense with a rearguard, and Baldwin barely managed to get away with the main army. Humphrey was killed. He had been one of Baldwin's last and truest friends.

Baldwin lived in constant pain now. His leprosy had advanced to the point where his face was hideously deformed. His hands and feet were shredding away. He put on a black veil to hide his face and covered his hands in the loose sleeves of his robe. More and more he became withdrawn. Raymond was in Tripoli. In 1180, Baldwin's old friend and tutor, William of Tyre, left for Europe to seek help for the crumbling kingdom. The only person left to befriend him in those days was his mother.

Agnes poured poisonous words in the young king's ear. She was anxious that Sibylla remarry—preferably to someone she could control. Sibylla had given birth to a boy, who had been christened Baldwin V, but the boy was sickly and might not live. The two women pestered the king endlessly, warning him of a nonexistent plot by Raymond of Tripoli to seize power. Under the constant pressure, his mind clouded by pain, Baldwin began to change. He became suspicious of his former friends. He quarreled with Raymond of Tripoli, and when William of Tyre returned from Europe, he found himself out of favor with the king. Then, in the spring of 1180, Agnes achieved her greatest victory. She found a husband for Sibylla, who suited them both in every way. He was a young man recently arrived from France with nothing to recommend him but his youth and good looks. His name was Guy of Lusignan.

Raymond was stunned when he returned from Tripoli to find Sibylla and Guy married, for he recognized Guy for what he was—a weak, spineless fool. The nomination of Guy as eventual regent for Baldwin V was followed by an even worse blunder, for it cost the king his last friend.

The patriarch of Jerusalem died in 1180. There was an obvious candidate for the job in William of Tyre, one of the most intelligent and able churchmen of the time. But Agnes was utterly opposed to William, partly because of his influence over the king and partly because of his friendship with her sworn enemy, Raymond of Tripoli. Agnes had her own candidate, a depraved cleric named Heraclius. He could barely read or write, but he had once been one of Agnes' lovers, and was, from all accounts, quite good looking. He currently kept an Italian mistress, the wife of a cloth merchant, in his quarters at Jerusalem.

William of Tyre begged the Church council not to elect Heraclius. He made a prophecy: "If he is elected, the city and all the kingdom will be lost." Heraclius became patriarch, and the tavern singers made songs about the new head of the Church and his "Madame Patriarch." Never since the days of the first patriarch, Arnulf, had the Church fallen so low.

Heraclius struck back at William quickly. In 1181, the archbishop of Tyre was excommunicated. William ended the history he had spent so many years writing and retired to Rome, where he died two years later under mysterious circumstances.

A two-year truce was arranged in 1180 between Baldwin and Saladin. Both sides desperately needed it. Saladin was still intent on capturing Aleppo. His defeat at Montisgard and his subsequent failures to destroy the army of the Franks had hurt his prestige. He needed Aleppo to unite all of Syria behind him.

The truce lasted a little over a year. Reynald of Chatillon had never intended to bide by it. In the summer of 1181, he raided a caravan traveling between Damascus and Mecca which had passed through his territory. Saladin angrily demanded that the stolen goods be returned. Baldwin agreed, in an attempt to keep the peace, but Reynald insolently refused. Short of outright civil war, there was nothing Baldwin could do. The war between Saladin and the Franks resumed.

For the next year, Baldwin rode at the head of his troops, raiding and fighting short skirmishes along the northern borders. Baldwin's actions kept the Muslims off balance, but he could not stave off the inevitable. In the summer of 1183, Saladin completed his conquest of Aleppo.

17

the horns of hattin

Reynald of Chatillon was a pirate at heart. Often in the past he had swooped down from his castle heights and plucked the rich caravans winding through his domains. His last raid had been a breach of the truce and had brought down the wrath of Saladin. But truces were for weaklings and cowards. Reynald was motivated by only two things: an insatiable greed and unwavering hatred for the Muslims. His sixteen years in a Muslim dungeon had driven him to the brink of madness.

But it was a calculated madness. Reynald was not a fool. He had safely defied the king because he had the support of the Templars and because his castle made him nearly invincible. Now, in the spring of 1183, he made another calculation, and prepared to launch his most ambitious project. Saladin was occupied at Aleppo and could not interfere. The king was at Nazareth, stricken with malaria. Reynald had been preparing for this moment for months. His men had constructed ships in the heart of the desert and carried them for miles overland to the tip of the Red Sea. Local pirates, attracted by promises of fabulous loot, had been enlisted as guides. Reynald meant to strike at the very heart of Islam.

Reynald joined his men at Aqaba, and his fleet sailed down the coast of Africa, raiding and burning ports as they went. Then they turned east and sailed toward the ports that served as gateways for Muslim pilgrims on their way to Mecca and Medina. The stunned Muslims put up a poor resistance at first. Reynald reached as far as ar-Raghih and sank a shipload of Muslim pilgrims. A merchant ship laden with treasure from India fell to him.

Saladin's brother, who was governing in Cairo, finally reacted. A Muslim fleet pursued and caught up with Reynald as he was making his way home. Most of the Christian fleet was captured or sunk, but Reynald escaped. Over a hundred captives were taken to Cairo and executed. Two were sent to Mecca, where they were beheaded in a special ceremony.

Reynald's rash invasion was certainly the act of a madman. The Muslim world recoiled from the outrage with horror. "People believed that the hour appointed for the last judgment and the end of the world had come," an Arab historian wrote. The Franks, who had been political pawns, were now seen as the instruments of the devil. The word which had not been heard since the time of Muhammad, and which had begun as a whisper and a hope in the mind of Saladin, rose in a frenzy that would sweep the Franks like dust into the sea. *Jihad*.

Holy War.

In the fall of 1183, Baldwin was dying. Even the young king seemed ready to acknowledge his own weakness. He lay at Nazareth, recovering from a fever that had drained the remaining strength from his body. He was nearly blind. The boy "who could ride a horse like a man" was no longer able to walk. He was carried now in a litter. The stench of rotting flesh rose from his body like the sign of a plague.

Even then, Baldwin was reluctant to surrender. His mother and sister urged him to retire and give the regency to Guy of Lusignan. Events were running away from Baldwin. His younger sister, Isabella, was to be married to the grandson of Humphrey of Toron at Reynald's castle of Kerak. Reynald himself had disappeared on some unknown project of his own. With misgivings, Baldwin agreed to retire. Guy was appointed regent.

Guy did not enjoy his new power long. While the king lay sick at Nazareth, Saladin entered the country once again, south of the Sea of Galilee. For once the Franks were assembled in strength and moved quickly to intercept him. Raymond of Tripoli was with the army, but Guy was in command. The Franks blundered into a trap near Mount Tabor. The army was surrounded in a narrow valley, and Saladin's forces kept them bottled up for eight days with no food and little water. Raymond advised Guy not to attack the superior Muslim force, which was exactly what Saladin was trying to provoke. Guy fumbled and hesitated. While part of Saladin's army guarded the Franks like sheep in a pen, the rest ravaged the countryside. Finally, Saladin retired toward Damascus, unmolested.

When Baldwin heard of the debacle at Tabor, he exploded. The incident seemed to give him new life. He stripped Guy of the regency and demanded that Sibylla divorce the fool. This Sibylla would not do. She traveled to Ascalon, where Guy was hiding, and joined her husband. Baldwin pursued the fugitives to the walls of Ascalon. The gates were slammed shut in the king's face. In a fury, Baldwin crawled from his litter and beat against the gates. The men inside simply laughed at him.

Guy's rebellion finally brought Baldwin to his senses. He realized that Jerusalem's last hope lay with the man he had believed to be his enemy. Baldwin and Raymond of Tripoli were reconciled. It was very nearly too late, for Saladin had by then heard of Reynald's latest outrage.

Saladin meant first to punish the criminal upstart. He swore that he would personally kill Reynald at the first opportunity. He was not yet prepared for a full-scale war. But he gathered his men in November, 1183, and marched toward Reynald's castle of Kerak. He arrived in time to interrupt a wedding.

Isabella and Humphrey of Toron were in the chapel when the sounds of fighting and the war cry of the Muslims sounded across the castle ramparts. The drawbridge was pulled up, and the castle garrison flew to the walls. The wedding continued.

Saladin had brought mangonels and siege engines, intending to pull the castle down stone by stone. It was evident, however, that there would be a long fight. Reynald's wife sent out servants from the castle with food and drink from the wedding feast. "We were not expecting visitors," she said, "or we could have provided better." Saladin asked where the young bride and her husband were staying. A tower was pointed out to him. Saladin ordered his men not to shoot at the tower. He would not disturb a couple newly married.

Despite the courtesies, the fight was deadly serious. The Franks had designed their castle well. Saladin made little progress. For a month the Muslims ripped at the walls and were answered in turn with fire and arrows. Then Saladin heard that the king of Jerusalem had risen from his bed and was leading the army of Jerusalem against him. Saladin abandoned the siege and retreated toward Damascus. The blind, crippled king had to be carried from his litter into the castle. He had routed his old enemy for the last time.

A little over a year later, Baldwin's agony came to an end. He called Raymond and the knights of Jerusalem to his bedside and dictated his will. The crown of Jerusalem must go to Sibylla's son, Baldwin V, with Raymond acting as regent. If little Baldwin died, Raymond must continue to rule until the pope and the crowned heads of Europe could select a new king. At all costs the crown must be kept from the inept Guy of Lusignan.

Raymond was fearful. He knew that Baldwin V was a sick child and probably would not live. But there seemed no other solution. Isabella's husband, Humphrey of Toron, had turned out almost as badly as Guy. People said of Humphrey, "He was more like a woman than a man." Raymond accepted Baldwin's wishes. The other knights swore to support him.

Baldwin the Leper died in March 1185, at the age of twenty-four. His body was wasted away and created no burden for the men who carried it to the Church of the Holy Sepulcher. Baldwin was laid beside Godfrey of Bouillon. Raymond and the crowd who mourned the king could not have known it at the time, but Baldwin's burial in the Holy Sepulcher was an appropriate and symbolic gesture. He was destined to be remembered as the last and possibly the greatest of its defenders.

In September 1186, Raymond's fears were realized. The child

king, Baldwin V, was dead. During the year and a half of
Raymond's regency, there had been peace. Raymond had persuaded Saladin to accept a five-year truce. The enthusiasm for a
holy war sparked by Reynald's attack on Mecca had waned.
Saladin had been bedridden with fever and had come close to
death himself. In those months, it was still possible that the
ultimate disaster could be averted.

With the death of Baldwin V, the last hope flickered out.
Raymond called a council at Nablus to determine the best way to
select a new king according to Baldwin IV's will. Humphrey of
Toron was there, along with the powerful knight Baliol of Ibelin,
who controlled the Galilee. The barons of the coastal cities all
attended. Only Reynald, Guy, and the Grand Masters of the
Military Orders were absent. They had hurried to Jerusalem in an
attempt to foil Raymond's plans.

Raymond wanted to crown Humphrey of Toron, but the
young man was terrified. He had no wish to be a king. For a while
the barons considered giving the crown directly to Raymond. He
had certainly proved himself worthy of it. Then came news from
Jerusalem. The barons had wasted too much time.

As soon as Baldwin V was buried, and as Raymond was calling
the council, Agnes of Courtenay and Sibylla and her husband met
with the patriarch, Heraclius, in Jerusalem. Reynald and Gerard
of Ridfort, Grand Master of the Templars, joined them. The
Templars shut the gates of the city, and Reynald's men occupied
the citadel. The Grand Master of the Hospitalers protested in
vain. Most of his men were with Raymond, and he was helpless
alone. Sibylla and her husband entered the Church of the Holy
Sepulcher, where Heraclius and several witnesses were waiting.
The patriarch had two crowns. He placed one of them on Sibylla's
head, and she was pronounced queen. "Now," said Heraclius,
"take the other crown and place it on the head of the man you
deem worthy to rule the kingdom." Sibylla took the crown and
turned to her husband. He knelt beside her, and the weight was
placed on his head. In a quick, bloodless revolution, Guy of
Lusignan had become king of Jerusalem.

The barons of Outremer were outraged. Raymond returned to
Tripoli and would not acknowledge the new king. Some of the

lesser nobles abandoned their lands around Jerusalem and went north to join Bohemond of Antioch. Even Guy's brother wondered at the folly. "By my faith," he was heard to say, "if they have made him a king, they should make me a god." The kingdom was split down the middle, with the Templars almost at war with the Hospitalers and the barons of the coastal cities ranged against the king's men in Jerusalem. The only thing between Jerusalem and final destruction was the truce with Saladin.

Guy meant to keep the truce. Even he was wise enough to know that peace was a way of buying time. Already there were stirrings in Europe for a fresh Crusade. Henry II of England had sent a token force to Outremer. He had promised to come himself at a later date. But Guy was saddled with an ally more dangerous than his enemies. Reynald of Chatillon had been the cause of one disaster after another, and at the end of 1186, he committed the final atrocity. Reynald joined with a tribe of Bedouins in attacking a caravan between Cairo and Damascus. The small Egyptian security force was killed. The merchants and women in the caravan were hauled away and locked in the dungeons of Kerak. One chronicler says that Saladin's sister was among the captives.

This time nothing could heal the breach. Saladin finally proclaimed the jihad. In Cairo, Aleppo, and Damascus, the Muslim armies gathered.

Raymond of Tripoli almost wept with frustration. He met with Saladin and swore he had no wish to make war. Saladin received him coldly. He agreed to keep peace with Raymond in exchange for safe passage across the count's lands. Raymond had no choice but to agree. His only hope now was to save his own country.

Guy bitterly denounced Raymond as a traitor. A few days later, Gerard headed toward Tripoli with the Grand Master of the Hospitalers and Baliol of Ibelin. They meant to try to make peace with Raymond and persuade him to join them in the face of the common danger. Baliol had to stop for a night at his own castle in Galilee, and the two Grand Masters rode ahead with about 150 knights. As they were approaching Tripoli, Raymond was meeting with representatives from Saladin. The Muslims were making a reconnaissance and had stopped to gain permission to cross Raymond's lands. Raymond gave them permission provided they spent only one day in his country and made no attacks on any towns or fortresses. The terms were strictly observed.

But the Muslims had said nothing about attacking knights in open combat. After they left Tripoli, they ran into the Templars and Hospitalers heading toward Tripoli on their peacekeeping mission.

The Muslim force numbered several thousand, most of them professional soldiers, the cream of Saladin's army. When the knights saw what they were up against, even the bravest suggested retreat. Gerard would not have it. He turned to his chief lieutenant and mocked him: "You love that blond head of yours too much to lose it." The insult and the rivalry between the two orders tipped the balance. The knights charged. It was typical of the gallantry of both orders. It was also suicide. Of the 150 knights, only three survived and escaped, bleeding and battered, to carry the news to Raymond. One of them was the Grand Master, Gerard.

Raymond was horrified by the slaughter he had indirectly caused. The truce with Saladin was over. Raymond met Guy and swore homage to him. The other deserters joined the cause. All the forces of Outremer gathered at Acre for the final showdown with Saladin. Even Reynald left his castle and was reconciled with Raymond.

The country was stripped of defenders. Two knights remained at Jerusalem. Raymond's wife commanded a civilian force at Tiberias on the Sea of Galilee. The coastal cities were similarly helpless. Heraclius was summoned from Jerusalem with the True Cross, but the patriarch declined the honor. The True Cross was entrusted to the bishop of Acre.

On July 1, 1187, Saladin crossed the Jordan River with 20,000 men. His first target was the city of Tiberias. He knew he would have to move fast. Tiberias was in the midst of desert country, and in the heat of summer he could not stand a long siege.

On the night of July 1, the Franks held a council. Raymond was cautious. He knew of Saladin's problem and believed the Muslims were inviting them into a trap. The next day the Franks camped on a hilltop a day's march from Tiberias. It was a perfect spot for defense. There was plenty of water and grass for the horses. That night a messenger from Tiberias reached the camp. The town had fallen, but Raymond's wife was holding out in the citadel.

Again a meeting was held, and again Raymond urged Guy to remain on the defensive. "I have more to lose than any of you," Raymond said. "It is my wife and my lands that are threatened, but I would rather lose them both than lose the kingdom."

Raymond's advice was sensible. Saladin's army stood between the Franks and the Sea of Galilee. There was no water for them if they left their position, and even one day without water could mean death for a man marching in heavy armor through the blast-furnace heat around Tiberias. Saladin must attack or withdraw. Either way he could be defeated. Guy listened to Raymond, but later the king was visited by Gerard. "Are we women?" the Templar asked pointedly. "Are you going to listen to a known traitor?" Guy's greatest problem was that he couldn't make up his mind. He let Gerard persuade him to lead the army toward Tiberias in the morning.

July 3 was stifling. The sun rose in a clear sky and beat against the long line of men marching down the road to Tiberias. By late afternoon, men were dropping, their throats parched and cracked from lack of water. They reached the sides of a small hill and made their camp because they could go no farther. Above them, the hill rose to two summits, one on each end. Between the summits the Sea of Galilee shimmered in the light of the setting sun. The place was called the Horns of Hattin.

There was a well at the place they camped, but it was dry. Raymond saw their position and cried, "God, it is already over. The battle is lost, and we are dead men." The exhausted Franks were visited during the night by the Muslim army, who pressed close to the hill. By morning the Franks were completely surrounded.

On the morning of July 4, the Franks had only one thought: water. The foot soldiers were the first to break. They were maddened by thirst, and the sight of the water in the distance pulled them. They were cut down like cattle. The wind was blowing toward the Franks, and Saladin ordered fire set to the brush. The flame and rolling clouds of smoke completed what thirst had begun.

The knights grouped together on the hill and repelled one Muslim charge after another. Their numbers dwindled steadily. The Franks retreated to the top of the Horns and made a desperate countercharge. It nearly broke through. Saladin, watching the battle with his son from a nearby hilltop, tugged at his beard and blanched. "Curse the Devil for a liar," he shouted. But the Frankish charge was broken and turned back.

It was over then. Guy fought courageously to the last. "We have routed them," Saladin's son shouted happily, but the tiny circle of knights held. Guy ordered Raymond and a few others to abandon the hill and try to break through. Raymond and Baliol of Ibelin made it with a handful of men. "Nothing could have withstood them," an Arab chronicler wrote of Raymond's desperate escape. "They fought like wolves."

The True Cross went down, and the bishop of Acre was killed. Again Saladin's son shouted, "We have routed them."

"Be quiet," Saladin replied. "The battle is not over as long as that flag stands." He pointed to Guy's standard, and as he spoke, the standard fell.

The king, Reynald of Chatillon, and the Grand Master of the Templars were taken captive. They no longer had the strength to lift their swords. The battlefield was littered with uncounted dead and wounded from both sides. A few of the surviving Frankish knights went to Saladin and begged permission to kill their wounded comrades. The screams of pain from thirst and gaping wounds were silenced. Guy's army had numbered several thousand men when it set out from Acre. Barely two hundred escaped the battle.

The king and Reynald were taken to Saladin's tent. Saladin was courteous. He asked Guy to sit and gave him a cup of water. Guy drank from it and handed the cup to Reynald. "Remember," Saladin said sharply, "it was you who offered him drink, not I."

Reynald finished the cup, and some of his old arrogance returned. Saladin stood up and faced him. The sultan reminded Reynald of his numerous crimes against Islam. "I simply traveled a well-worn path," Reynald replied.

"Will you accept Islam?" Saladin demanded.

Reynald laughed contemptuously. Saladin brought his sword

down on Reynald's neck and shoulder. A servant finished him off. Reynald's body was pitched from his tent.

Guy saw what had happened. He thought he was next. He nearly fainted. "Do not worry," Saladin said to him. "That man had passed all limits. But kings are not in the habit of killing kings."

Perhaps there was satisfied irony in Saladin's voice. Guy was no longer a king; there was no longer a kingdom.

18

help for
the holy sepulcher

Saladin's final revenge was reserved for the Templars and Hospitalers. About three hundred had been captured after the Battle of Hattin. Saladin paid their captors fifty gold pieces for each of them, then invited his men to try out their swords on the heads of the warrior monks. As usual each man was offered the opportunity to convert to Islam. When they refused, as all of them did, their heads rolled in the dust. Only one man was spared—the Grand Master, Gerard of Ridfort. Saladin had a use for him.

After this atrocity, there were no more reprisals. Saladin proved to be a surprisingly gentle conqueror. The regular knights and other captives were spared. Many were later ransomed.

The day after Hattin, Saladin began his final conquest. The escape by Raymond of Tripoli annoyed him, for it made his victory incomplete. But all the Frankish holdings lay open before him, and Raymond could not be a serious threat.

In fact he was not. The count of Tripoli made his way back to his own city, but he was a broken man. He never recovered, and he never raised his sword against the Muslims again. He died within a few months—it was said, of despair.

The other escapee was to prove tougher. Baliol of Ibelin rode to

Jerusalem, and the population rode up to greet him with cries for help. The situation seemed hopeless. With Baliol's arrival the total number of knights in the city rose to three. There were a few squires and men-at-arms, and thousands of refugees swelling the city. At first Baliol wished nothing more than to ensure an honorable surrender. He listened to the clamoring of the crowd, and he calmed them. "We will fight," he said.

Baliol asssembled all the men and boys of noble family left in the city over the age of fifteen. He knighted them all in a hasty ceremony. The remaining civilians—butchers, merchants, craftsmen, and monks—hastened to take up arms. In the moment of peril they seemed to remember it was not just their country they were fighting for, but the holy places. For the first time in eighty years, something of the fire that had burned in the pilgrims of the first Crusade was ignited again.

Saladin knew nothing of this. He was busy rolling up the countryside. Tiberias surrendered on July 5. Acre negotiated a surrender on the eighth, and Saladin entered the city on the tenth. Most of the towns and fortresses in the Galilee put up no resistance. Sidon and Beirut gave out by the end of the month. Tyre, the city that had resisted the Crusaders for twenty-four years, had to be bypassed. By the middle of September, all the towns in the former kingdom of Jerusalem, except a few isolated castles like Montreal and Kerak and the cities of Tyre and Jerusalem, were in Muslim hands. Tripoli and Antioch were not immediately threatened.

On September 20, Saladin set up his camp on the north side of Jerusalem's wall. By the twenty-sixth, his engineers were pounding a hole in the wall near the spot where Godfrey of Bouillon had broken into the city. The Muslims met fierce resistance. The Arab chroniclers later expressed surprise. It had not occurred to them that the Christians might look on Jerusalem with the same ardor that the Muslims felt for Mecca. After eighty-eight years, there was still no understanding between the two sides.

By the thirtieth, the engineers had torn a great hole in the wall. The Muslim army swarmed through. The Franks fought with desperate fury. At nightfall the Muslims had been thrown back, and the breach was plugged. Baliol had ordered that secondary defenses be constructed through the city, and every street blocked with barricades. He knew the resistance was hopeless. Under a flag of truce, he visited Saladin's tent to ask for terms.

"I mean to take Jerusalem the same way the Christians took it from us," Saladin told Baliol. "I will take it with a sword. The men will die, and the women will go into slavery."

Baliol understood. "We know we cannot hold out against you," he said. "When we see your men coming against us, we will kill our women and children with our own hands. We will destroy every mosque in the city and set fire to the rest. Not one animal will be left to serve you. And when the city is a heap of ruins, we will come out against you, and not one of us will survive. You may win, but you will inherit a desert."

Saladin listened to Baliol's speech and was troubled by it. He knew the knight was speaking the literal truth. Saladin was not a cruel man. He asked for Baliol's terms. "Only that our lives be spared, and the people be allowed to pay a ransom."

Saladin agreed but the price was steep. For every man the price was ten gold pieces, five for a woman, and one for a child. For those unable to pay, a lump sum of 100,000 gold pieces must be gathered. It was an impossible demand. For every man in the city there were fifty women, refugees from the disaster at Hattin. None of them had any money.

On the morning of October 2, thousands of people lined up at the gates of the city. As each passed through, a handful of coins was given to the Muslim guards. The treasury of the Templars ransomed 7,000 poor people, but Heraclius remained in character to the end. He paid his ten gold pieces and rode out of the city accompanied by a packhorse laden with gold. He refused to donate any of it to the poor. When all the ransoms were paid and there was no money left in the city, 20,000 poor people remained. Saladin's brother came to him and offered to give up his share of the spoils of the war in return for a thousand captives. As soon as the request was granted, he set the captives free.

The humane gesture sparked others. Saladin released all the remaining old men and women, and all the children. Two old men came to Saladin and asked that they be allowed to stay in the city. They were bent with age and could hardly have survived the aimless exodus that poured from the gates. One said he had come to Jerusalem as a boy in the service of Godfrey of Bouillon. The other had served with Baldwin I. Saladin gladly allowed them to remain.

The remaining refugees departed the city by passing through the low postern gate of St. Lazarus. They joined the stream and they wept. The bells of the city tolled emptily behind them. They did not weep for themselves, but for something intangible—something that was priceless and could not be ransomed.

The refugees streamed into Tyre and Tripoli and Antioch. They swelled the cities to the bursting point. And they saw that their gallant defense of Jerusalem was a beginning. The stunning shock of Hattin had given way to anger. A nucleus was growing, and it found its expression in a new cry that would sweep Europe and bring, at last, the fury of the kings: "Help! Help for the Holy Sepulcher!"

From out of the north a ship plowed through the choppy waters of the Mediterranean toward Acre. On board were several hundred knights and an Italian baron named Conrad of Montferrat. Conrad was the brother of William Longsword, the ill-fated knight who had married Sibylla of Jerusalem so many years before. Conrad had accompanied his brother as far as Constantinople, and like many others he had stayed and fallen in love with the city on the Bosporus. For many years he had served as a mercenary in the army of the Byzantine emperor. Now, in the summer of 1187, he was making his way to Jerusalem to fulfill his vows.

On July 14, Conrad's ship sailed into the harbor at Acre. The pink walls of the city glowed in the morning sun, and there was no sign of unusual activity. But Conrad sensed that something was wrong. The banners on the towers were unfamiliar, and there was no welcoming throng on the docks. Conrad ordered the ship's captain to stand away from land and hold the anchor. Soon a small boat put out from the dock. The men on board were Arabs.

Conrad hailed the boat and told the Arabs he was a merchant from Constantinople. He asked if there was any news. The Arabs excitedly told him of the battle at Hattin and of Saladin's conquests. Acre had been in Muslim hands for four days.

Something in Conrad's face gave him away. "This is no merchant," someone said, and the Arabs turned to raise the alarm. The captain of the Christian ship cast off and left Acre under full sail. Conrad had narrowly avoided capture. He tacked up the coast to Tyre and immediately began building a defense.

Conrad was the leader the men of Tyre were waiting for. His several hundred knights strengthened the city considerably. Conrad was not suffering from the demoralizing aftereffects of Hattin. He was one of the few men that summer who still believed Saladin could be defeated. Because of Conrad's presence, Saladin chose to bypass Tyre in his triumphant march along the coast. In the fall, after the capture of Jerusalem, Saladin returned to Tyre again.

Saladin had expected a fight, but he had not expected the furious resistance he met now. Many of the refugees from Jerusalem had gone to Tyre, and the stories they told of Baliol of Ibelin's defense inspired the new Crusaders who had come with Conrad. In November, Saladin threw the full weight of his army against Tyre, but Conrad drove him back with heavy losses. Saladin cursed the mistake he had made in not taking the city in the summer. Now it was too late. The Muslim army was exhausted by the long campaign. The rains were coming. Many of Saladin's men were anxious to return home for the winter. They had already accomplished great things.

Reluctantly, Saladin let about half his army disband. A small force was left to keep watch over Tyre, and the rest continued the mopping-up campaign. The outlying fortresses of Tripoli and Antioch fell, but Krak des Chevaliers, the immense Hospitaler castle, was impregnable. Montreal and Kerak held out for over a year and finally surrendered only because the defenders were on the verge of starvation.

By the summer of 1188, it was clear to Saladin that the Franks were still too strong to be completely eliminated. The best he could do was keep up a steady pressure and strike at their weak points. He knew, too, that the greatest weakness of the Crusaders was their own political ambitions. Conrad of Montferrat was already being hailed as their new king by the men of Tyre. So in the summer of 1188, Saladin shrewdly decided to release his prisoners—among them, the king of Jerusalem, Guy of Lusignan.

Saladin's calculations proved correct. Guy was no sooner released than the Franks were split down the middle. Guy and Sibylla first attempted to join the defenders of Tyre. Conrad ordered the gates of the city shut against them. "You have sacrificed all claim to the title of king," Conrad told Guy. The humiliated king had no choice but to move on to Tripoli. There he sat for nearly a year and brooded.

Saladin was prevented from continuing his conquests during the winter and spring of 1189 by a severe attack of malaria. The disease not only weakened and demoralized him, it gave the Crusaders what they needed more than anything—time. Saladin knew that fresh armies were gathering in Europe. Spies brought him news and rumors from Tyre, and the news was disquieting. It seemed that all of Europe was on the march.

This time there was no need for oratory to provoke enthusiasm for a new Crusade. Every man who heard of the loss of Jerusalem felt the news like a personal blow. Jerusalem had been a part of Western Christendom for so long that even the common people of England and France reacted as if their own countries were being invaded.

Frederick Barbarossa, the emperor of Germany, was the first of the monarchs to take the cross. He was a man nearly seventy years old, but he had an almost mystical power over his people. He had been one of the few with Conrad of Germany who had survived the massacre of 1147. The experience had taught him much. He began to assemble an army of 50,000 men, with no civilians or women to slow them down.

In England, the aging king, Henry II, was finally stirring. Henry was at war with Philip II of France and not particularly anxious to abandon his country for an uncertain venture in the East. But public and papal pressure were too much for him. His own soldiers were ready to desert him for the cause of the Holy Sepulcher. Philip was facing the same kind of ultimatum. In the early part of 1188, the two kings made peace and swore to retake Jerusalem. Henry was not able to fulfill his promise. He died the following year, and his crown and his vows were taken up by his oldest surviving son, Richard.

While the French and English kings were keeping a cautious eye on each other and building up their forces, men from Italy, Denmark, Sicily, and Norway were sailing toward the coast of Palestine in a continuous flood. They landed at Tripoli and Tyre, and they hurried south, where they heard the sounds of a growing battle.

By the summer of 1189, Guy of Lusignan had been joined at Tripoli by two hundred knights and several hundred foot soldiers, most of them new arrivals from the West. Guy decided that only a spectacular gesture or a stunning victory over Saladin could restore his title and prestige. So Guy set out with his two hundred knights to challenge Saladin and lay siege to the city of Acre.

When Saladin heard of Guy's movement, he couldn't believe it. He was certain the attack was a diversion of some sort. Guy soon made it clear he was serious. His men made camp on a small hill east of Acre. They dug trenches around their camp to neutralize the Muslim cavalry and diverted a stream to create a moat around their position. By the time Saladin realized the Crusaders really meant to besiege Acre, they were firmly dug in. Saladin arrived with his army in early October and assaulted the trenches. Guy's two hundred knights had been reinforced by a steady trickle of Danes, Norwegians, and Italians. The new Crusaders fought with determination. Saladin was forced to withdraw.

Through the fall and winter the Crusader army grew. Conrad came down from Tyre with thousands of new men from the West. Saladin called in his dispersed forces. The Crusaders would not budge from their positions in front of Acre, and Saladin dared not attack the massed army of the Franks. So the battle turned into a stalemate. The Crusader camp formed a ring around the land side of Acre. The camp was ringed, in turn, by squadrons of Saladin's cavalry.

There were continual skirmishes and truces. The Muslims inside Acre were supplied and reinforced by sea. They would sometimes venture out of the city in small groups, harassing stragglers at the edge of the camp, then retreating back behind their walls. But the winter rains had started, and in the sea of mud that engulfed the camp, neither side was ready to fight the decisive battle. In the spring, the galleys of Genoa and Pisa arrived to cut off the sea approaches to the city. A sea battle raged for days across the mouth of the harbor, and in the end the Egyptian fleet limped away. New galleys from the West beached on the shore, carrying men and supplies to the struggle.

A vast city of tents and mud-filled trenches was growing in front of Acre. From the walls of Acre, the camp looked like an immense garbage dump strewed across the land. When the rains stopped, flies rose in clouds, and they brought unheard-of diseases. An epidemic raged through the camp in the summer of 1190, and thousands of men and women died in the space of a few weeks. But the men besieging the city did not despair. In that same summer, they heard that the German emperor and his 50,000 knights and men-at-arms had left Constantinople and were crossing the wastelands of Asia Minor.

They marched in tight formation, past Dorylaeum, through the trackless hills of Cilicia, and the Turks pulled away from them. Part of the reason was simple prudence. The Turks had never faced a crusading army as large or as well disciplined as this one. Another part was the Seljuks' fear of Saladin. The king of Cairo and Damascus had grown too powerful and needed a check from the Franks. So the army of Crusaders passed unmolested until they reached a river near the Cilician Gates. Frederick's horse entered the chilly water and slipped. Frederick was thrown. The shock was too much for the old man. Within a few days he was dead.

The great army of the Germans, which had been held together by Frederick's leadership, broke up. Most went home. A few thousand determined men continued south with Frederick's son, but he had neither the personality nor the forces to cow the Muslims. Harassed daily by Saladin's cavalry, they straggled into the camp at Acre. Barely 2,000 out of the original 50,000 were left.

The Franks at Acre reacted to Frederick's death by attacking with new fury. There were no more truces. Eight thousand Franks died in a single day in an attack on Saladin's camp. The pressure on the walls of Acre grew. The Crusaders built engines of wood and iron, some of which could sling uprooted tree trunks across the ramparts of the city. The Muslims answered by burning the engines—for there was a man in the city who knew the secret of Greek fire.

As the number of Crusaders grew, famine added to the misery in the camp. Another fall and winter passed, and still the walls of Acre stood unbroken. In the spring of 1191, Philip of France arrived. Philip was an expert at siege warfare, but what the Crusaders needed was a man to lead them in an assault. After two years it was obvious that Acre could only be taken by swords at close quarters. In the summer of 1191, the man arrived. He was Richard I of England, a knight so renowned for his courage that already men were calling him Coeur-de-Lion—the Lion Heart.

19

the crusade of the kings

Richard had been a long time coming. It had been nearly four years since the king of Jerusalem's banner fell at Hattin and the Muslims entered Acre. There were reasons for the delay. The death of Henry and the drawn-out negotiations with Philip of France had occupied Richard until the summer of 1190. Another six months had been wasted in Sicily, where Richard's widowed sister Joanna had been disputing with the king of Sicily over her husband's inheritance. By the spring of 1191, Richard had finally set sail for Palestine, but a storm had scattered his fleet. The remnants washed up on the shores of Cyprus, and there Richard found new excuses for delay.

One of the ships at Cyprus carried Joanna and Richard's intended bride, Berengaria of Navarre. The Byzantine governor of the island invited them to his palace, but they were suspicious of the governor's motives. They feared they would be held for ransom. They refused to leave the ship. Angrily, the governor cut off supplies of food and water. When Richard arrived a few days later, he was furious at the insult. Richard's revenge was swift. He was joined at Cyprus by distinguished visitors—Guy of Lusignan and Humphrey of Toron. With their help, Richard conquered all of Cyprus in a matter of days. The Byzantine governor was bound and imprisoned in silver chains.

Richard was properly grateful to Guy for his help, and promised to support the king in his bid for the throne of Jerusalem. It was support Guy desperately needed. His claim was growing increasingly slender. The previous October Sibylla had died of the plague in the camp outside Acre, and Isabella had been forced into divorcing Humphrey of Toron. She was now married to Conrad of Montferrat.

Richard's meddling in the politics of Outremer was almost to prove his undoing. It was typical of the English king's arrogance, and it drove a further wedge between the leaders of the Crusade even before his arrival. Philip was a strong supporter of Conrad, as were most of the barons and kings who had taken the cross. The dispute was postponed by the immediate task of capturing Acre. Richard arrived on June 7 and was welcomed by a vast throng of soldiers from all nations. Even Philip offered his hand, but his welcome was a grudging one. A quip was already circulating around the camp: "The English king has the heart of a lion; the French king has the heart of a lamb."

Richard's happy welcome was short-lived. The day after his arrival, Richard failed to emerge from his tent. He had been struck by the fever that had already killed thousands of Crusaders, including Philip's cousin. The disease seemed to resist all treatment; it simply had to run its course with high fevers and blister sores that broke across the mouth and throat until the victim recovered or died. Richard was young and in perfect health when he arrived. Yet he hovered near death for days.

In the Muslim camp, Saladin also knew of Richard's arrival and his illness. Saladin had been wracked by fever himself, which prevented him from leading his men into battle. He knew the English king's reputation, and he offered a rare gesture of respect. Gifts of snow and fresh fruit were sent by Saladin to Richard's tent to ease the fever. And Richard recovered. Two weeks after his arrival, Richard was carried from his tent to the battle line, where he could watch the progress of his men.

The focus of the battle now centered on a corner of the wall which the Crusaders called the Accursed Tower. Philip's engineers had been steadily mining under the tower, and on a hot morning in early July, piles of brush and logs carried into the cavern dug under the tower were set alight. The heat split the stones; the tower cracked, tipped, and nearly collapsed. But it did not fall. Richard, watching from his command post, offered four gold pieces to any man who would brave the Muslim arrows and bring him a stone from the tower. Dozens died in the attempt, and still the tower stood. Unable to endure the waiting, Richard took a crossbow himself, and though he was still too weak to stand, began firing bolts against the men on the ramparts.

The Accursed Tower fell at last, and the weary Crusaders made one last assault. They were turned back in a holocaust of Greek fire, but the defenders of Acre had exhausted their strength. On July 12, the city surrendered.

Saladin had tried to prevent the surrender, but his messenger was too late. He sat in his tent without sleeping the night of the surrender, and the next day he met with Richard's envoys to discuss terms. Richard demanded a payment of 200,000 gold pieces for the ransom of the Muslim garrison, the release of all Christian prisoners, and the return of the True Cross captured at Hattin. Saladin agreed to the terms, but protested he would have difficulty raising so much money. He was given one month to come up with the first third.

That month, which should have been a time of triumph for the Crusaders, instead became a time of petty quarrels and dismal inactivity. On the day of his entrance into Acre, Richard sparked one of the most bitter and long-lasting of the quarrels himself. King Leopold of Austria, whose men had distinguished them-selves all through the battle, had his banner raised next to Richard's atop the royal palace in Acre. Richard ordered the banner struck. Someone cut Leopold's flag and threw it into a gutter.

The insult was unforgivable. Leopold resigned from the Crusade and went home with all his men. Two weeks later Philip of France also went home. Richard was left as undisputed head of the army, but it was an army whose morale had been broken. In two years nearly 80,000 men had died in the siege—most from disease. The survivors saw their leaders nearly at war with each other, and the natural hatreds between French and English, Germans and Flemings were revived. The only thing that could unite them again was a common cause, and the only common cause remaining was Jerusalem.

Perhaps that explains Richard's next action; at least it has been offered as an excuse. After a month of waiting, Richard was impatient. He could not afford to delay his march to Jerusalem, and Saladin was slow in coming up with the ransom payment. On August 20, Richard decided to wait no longer. The captured Muslims were gathered together and led to a field outside Acre. There, in full view of the Muslim camp, they were systematically massacred. The slaughter of the Muslim garrison permanently tarnished Richard's reputation, but at the time most chroniclers considered the action necessary. Richard could not afford to leave a strong Muslim force behind, even in captivity. Nevertheless it was a clear violation of the surrender terms. Saladin, in contrast, took no reprisals. The Christian captives were left unharmed; but Saladin swore he would take no more prisoners.

Two days after the massacre, Richard began his march south. Instead of moving directly inland toward Jerusalem, the army kept close to the coast. They were dependent on ships for their supply, and the sea protected their flank. Saladin's army followed on a parallel course, keeping out of sight behind the coastal hills.

Richard's first goal was Jaffa, the port city which controlled the approaches to Jerusalem. The army made slow progress. The terrain was difficult, cut by deep gulleys, and impeded by thick brush hiding scorpions and snakes. In their heavy armor, the Crusaders suffered more from the heat than from Muslim arrows. Saladin's cavalry and archers kept a constant pressure on the Crusaders' flank, killing dozens of stragglers daily. But Richard, who was well aware of the Muslim tactics, had devised an ingenious method of dealing with them. He divided his men into three columns. The inner column consisted of the baggage and hospital wagons, the second of the knights with their horses, and the outside column was formed by the infantry. The infantry thus bore the brunt of the Muslim attacks, but the horses, who were most vulnerable to Muslim arrows, were protected.

Two weeks of marching brought the Crusader army to Arsuf

(on the coast of Israel between Tel Aviv and Netanya), and there Saladin had prepared what he hoped would be the decisive battle. On the morning of September 7, the Crusader camp began its usual order of march, with the Templars in the lead and the Hospitalers guarding the rear. Saladin's attack fell first on the Hospitalers, who were hard pressed and under orders not to charge no matter what the provocation. Richard rode up and down the line steadying his men. The leader of the Hospitalers came to him begging permission to counterattack. Richard wanted to hold back a little longer, but the decision was taken out of his hands. Two knights in the rearguard broke from the line and galloped toward the Muslim lines, their lances down. Within moments, the rest of the knights were after them. Richard gave the signal for a headlong charge.

The battle raged thoughout the day, with Richard always in the front line. One witness described the king "cutting a wide path for himself, like a reaper with his sickle. Everywhere the enemy gave him wide room."

Saladin was forced to retreat, and Richard entered Jaffa. He found the town abandoned and the walls nearly destroyed. But he could count the battle a clear victory—the first for the Crusaders in open combat since Hattin. Out of the Battle of Arsuf grew a legend of the red-haired king the Muslims called Malich-Ric—a name Muslim parents used to frighten troublesome children for many years after the "demon" had left their country and the Crusaders were all but forgotten.

But Richard could not move on Jerusalem for many weeks after the capture of Jaffa. The time was spent repairing the walls of the ruined city, and Saladin sent negotiators to the Crusader camp with orders to discuss a treaty—and stall for time.

During the negotiations, Saladin built up the defenses of Jerusalem and destroyed the fortress of Ascalon, which he could neither defend nor allow to fall into Crusader hands. Richard was beginning to realize that an attack on Jerusalem would probably be even more difficult than the siege of Acre. Nevertheless, the pressure from the men in the army forced him to take the field again in December 1191. The Crusaders approached within twelve miles of the Holy City, but then Richard ordered a retreat. At that moment, the Crusade was virtually at an end.

There were more battles. Saladin retook Jaffa for a time, but was driven out by Richard. There was another march toward Jerusalem in the summer of 1192, which ended like the first, in a retreat without a battle. The trouble was, Richard seemed to have lost interest in crusading. Part of the reason was the troublesome news he had received from England, where his brother John was ruling in his absence. Another part was the political defeat he suffered in the spring of 1192 at the hands of the native Franks.

The problem of the title of king of Jerusalem had still not been settled. In one sense it was an empty title, since it was becoming clear that Jerusalem was destined to remain in the hands of the Muslims. But the two disputants still fought with bitter words. In April 1192, a conference was held with all the native barons in attendance. They were asked to choose for the last time between Guy of Lusignan and Conrad of Montferrat as their king. Almost unanimously, they elected Conrad.

Richard made no secret of his displeasure, but he had to abide by the decision. As consolation, Richard offered Guy the island of Cyprus. Guy, as it turned out, had the best of the deal. He founded a long line of kings on Cyprus, and Conrad survived his election by only a few days. Conrad was murdered on the streets of Tyre by two members of a fanatical Muslim sect known as the Assassins.

Conrad's death was a terrible blow to the hopes of the Franks in Palestine. By his quick action at Tyre, he had saved a remnant of the kingdom, and there is no doubt that he would have been a worthy successor to the kings of Jerusalem. Neither Richard nor Saladin grieved for him. Isabella, at the age of twenty-one, was married for the third time, to a French knight named Henry of Champagne. Through her, the kings of Jerusalem continued to rule their shadowy kingdom from Acre for many years.

Richard's negotiations with Saladin ended in September with a guaranteed five-year truce. Jerusalem was opened to Christian pilgrims, but it remained under Muslim rule. The narrow coastal strip from Jaffa to Antioch was all that remained of the former kingdom.

Richard left for home in October, but he promised Saladin, "I shall return some day to conquer the Holy Land."

It was a hollow boast, and both men seemed to know it. "If I must lose Jerusalem," Saladin responded, "there is no one I would rather lose it to than the English king."

So it was ended. The Crusade of the Kings had come out of the West, in the words of an Arab chronicler, "like a mountain on the move, a sea of tumbling foaming waves." And like the sea it had crashed and broken and finally come to nothing along the shores of Palestine.

20

the last days

Richard did not keep his promise. On the way home, he had to pass through the lands belonging to Leopold of Austria. Richard realized the danger and made the journey disguised as a poor pilgrim. He was recognized at an inn, and Leopold had his revenge for the insult at Acre. Richard spent the next two years of his life languishing in an Austrian prison. After his release, Richard continued his wars—against Philip and against a rebellious vassal in Normandy. There he was killed by an arrow fired from the castle wall he was besieging.

Saladin survived the end of the crusade by only six months. His battles with disease and with the Franks had worn him out. The body of the great Muslim leader was carried through the streets of Damascus with a herald reading an epitaph Saladin had ordered for himself: "See all that remains of the glory of a conquering king."

The Crusades did not end then. For many years the ideal of the crusading knight fighting in the service of Christ continued to burn in Europe. But as time went on, and Jerusalem remained firmly in the hands of the Muslims, the ideal became blunted and turned to coarser uses.

In 1202, Pope Innocent III preached a new Crusade, but it was taken over by the merchant princes of Venice and turned against their archrival Constantinople. The thing that Alexius had feared from the first moment he saw the Crusaders in 1097 finally came to pass. Constantinople was conquered and ruled by Latins for over a hundred years.

The fifth Crusade was diverted to Egypt in 1218 and scored some early successes. Once again, it was personal ambition that led to the breakup of the Crusade when it seemed that it was on the verge of victory.

None of these Crusades affected the tiny kingdom clinging precariously to the coast of Palestine, with one exception. In 1227, the grandson of Frederick Barbarossa, Frederick II of Germany, launched what has been called the sixth Crusade. It was a Crusade that began with Frederick's excommunication and ended with the restoration of Jerusalem. Frederick was a scholarly man who spoke six languages, including Arabic. He was devoted to philosophy, the study of mathematics, and his own pleasure. He cared nothing for kings or popes, and is reported to have said once, "Moses, Christ, and Muhammad were all frauds."

At the time Frederick set out for the Holy Land, the sultan of Egypt and the sultan of Damascus were at war. Frederick began a correspondence with the sultan of Egypt and offered an alliance against Damascus in return for the restoration of Jerusalem. In fact, Frederick's offer was a gigantic bluff. He had no army of his own, and the barons of Outremer despised him. They were not about to involve themselves. Amazingly, Frederick's bluff worked. The sultan of Damascus died at a critical moment, and the sultan of Egypt kept his promise. Jerusalem was handed over to the Franks without a battle. Frederick's "conquest" lasted seventeen years.

The last great Crusade, the seventh, was led by Louis IX of France in 1248. Louis was a saintly man and was canonized shortly after his death in 1270. But he was utterly hopeless as a general. His attack on the Egyptians at Damietta (Dumyat) ended with his capture along with most of his army. The staggering ransom demanded by the sultan of Egypt almost broke the treasury of France and ended the crusading spirit in Europe for good.

Those years were a time of civil war and petty feudal squabbles in Outremer. Templars fought Hospitalers; rival merchants from the Italian cities fought with each other; and the landowning barons fought with everybody. Only the equally disruptive anarchy among the Muslims kept the Franks from being swept away forever.

In 1244, a new force had appeared in the East. A tribe of Turks, which had ridden down from the steppes of Asia, rolled over Jerusalem, plundering and slaughtering everyone they encountered. They were refugees from the Mongol invasions in the north. Because of those invasions, the Franks and the Muslims were united again—but the Muslims had by far the superior force. The descendants of Saladin were ousted by a new line of sultans, the Mamelukes, and it was they who brought about the final destruction of the Frankish kingdoms.

It took a long time. Jaffa and Antioch fell to the Mameluke Baybars in 1268. Tripoli fell in 1289, and in the spring of 1291, the last great battle was fought over Acre. After a month-long siege, Acre was left a smoking ruin. Templars and Hospitalers fought side by side in the last battle, but it was too late. No help came from Europe. Within a few days, Tyre, Beirut, and Sidon were abandoned. The exhausted refugees gathered at Cyprus. And Outremer faded into memory.

They seem very remote now, these men and women of Outremer. Eight hundred years have passed since a leper boy ruled his crumbling kingdom in Jerusalem. The past recedes faster now. Forty generations. Or, if you look at it in terms of lifetimes, laid end to end, only twelve. So perhaps they are not so remote after all. Certainly the questions that plagued them still continue to be raised, and the answers are as remote in the twentieth century as they were in the twelfth.

For the battles continue. Those who insist on finding either irony or justice in history might reflect that the people who were the first victims of the Crusaders have become, in a sense, their heirs. The motives may be different, but there are some similarities. Both Israel and Outremer were states founded out of a religious heritage, and they faced the same enemies and the same isolation. Outremer foundered after less than a century.

But the questions raised by the Crusades really concern more than Muslims, Christians, and Jews. The Crusades have been analyzed, debated over, condemned, and praised. Were they simply the last convulsive gasp of a barbarian age? Or were they the expression of the highest ideals of Western man—when thousands gave up home, property, and life in pursuit of an intangible goal? Is it possible to hold ideals without fighting for them? Or does the fighting somehow negate the ideals? Both answers to those questions have their supporters, and both can arrange the evidence to suit themselves. And perhaps both are right, for the fact remains that the men committed to the highest ideals of the Crusade also committed the worst atrocities at the moment of their fulfillment.

It may be that there is no final, absolute answer. But the questions must be asked. For the answers we give may well determine our own fate.

BIBLIOGRAPHY

ORIGINAL SOURCES

Fulcher of Chartres, *A History of the Expedition to Jerusalem, 1095–1127*. Translated by Francis Rita Ryan. Edited by Harold S. Fink. New York, W. W. Norton, 1969.

Gabrieli, Francesco (ed.), *Arab Historians of the Crusades*. Translated by E. J. Costello. Berkeley, Calif., University of California Press, 1969.

Krey, August C. (ed.), *The First Crusade: Accounts of Eye-Witnesses and Participants*. Magnolia, Maine, Peter Smith.

Peters, Edward (ed.), *The First Crusade: The Chronicle of Fulcher of Chartres and Other Source Materials*. Philadelphia, University of Pennsylvania Press, 1971.

William of Tyre, *A History of Deeds Done Beyond the Sea*. Translated by E. A. Babcock and A. C. Krey. New York, Columbia University Press, 1943.

SECONDARY SOURCES

Bradford, Ernle, *The Sword and the Scimitar: The Saga of the Crusades*. New York, G. P. Putnam's Sons, 1974.

169

Boase, T. S. R., *Kingdoms and Strongholds of the Crusaders.* New York, Bobbs-Merrill, 1971.

Lamb, Harold, *The Crusades.* Vol. I, *Iron Men and Saints.* New York, Garden City Publishing Co., 1930.

——Vol. II, *The Flame of Islam.*

Oldenbourg, Zoe, *The Crusades.* Translated by Anne Carter. New York, Pantheon Books, 1966.

Pernoud, Regine, *The Crusaders.* London, 1963.

Prawer, Joshua, *The Crusaders' Kingdom.* New York, Praeger, 1972.

Runciman, Steven, *A History of the Crusades.* Vol. I, *The First Crusade.* Cambridge, Cambridge University Press, 1962.

——Vol. II, *The Kingdom of Jerusalem.*

——Vol. III, *The Kingdom of Acre.*

Setton, Kenneth M. (ed.), *A History of the Crusades.* Vol. I, *The First Hundred Years.* Originally published Philadelphia, University of Pennsylvania Press, 1955.

index

171